BUTCH PATRICK'S
MUNSTER MEMORIES
A MINI COFFIN TABLE BOOK

Book Compiled and Designed by

RICHARD MAURIZIO
and
DEREK SHIMODA

Edited by

KEN WHEATON

Special Thanks to

KEVIN BURNS
TONY GRECO
MARK DOYLE

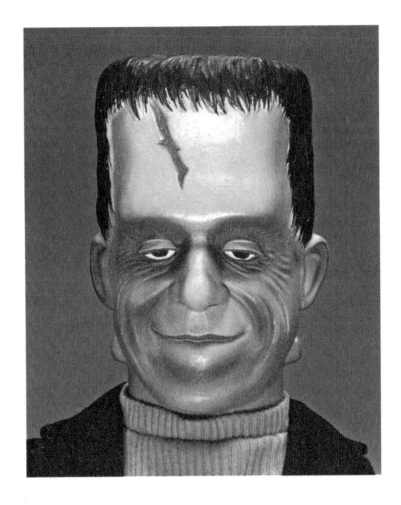

This book is an unauthorized edition and is intended to educate
the readers about this television show and celebrate its fifty years.

New Edition by TV Classics Press 2015
A Division of Micro Publishing Media, Inc.

This book is dedicated to all the fans who have kept the spirit
of this television show alive for fifty years.

Herman Munster
Measures 4' x 4'. Painted with acrylic and enamel on Masonite.
Painted by neo-pop artist and comic book creator - CHRIS YAMBAR.

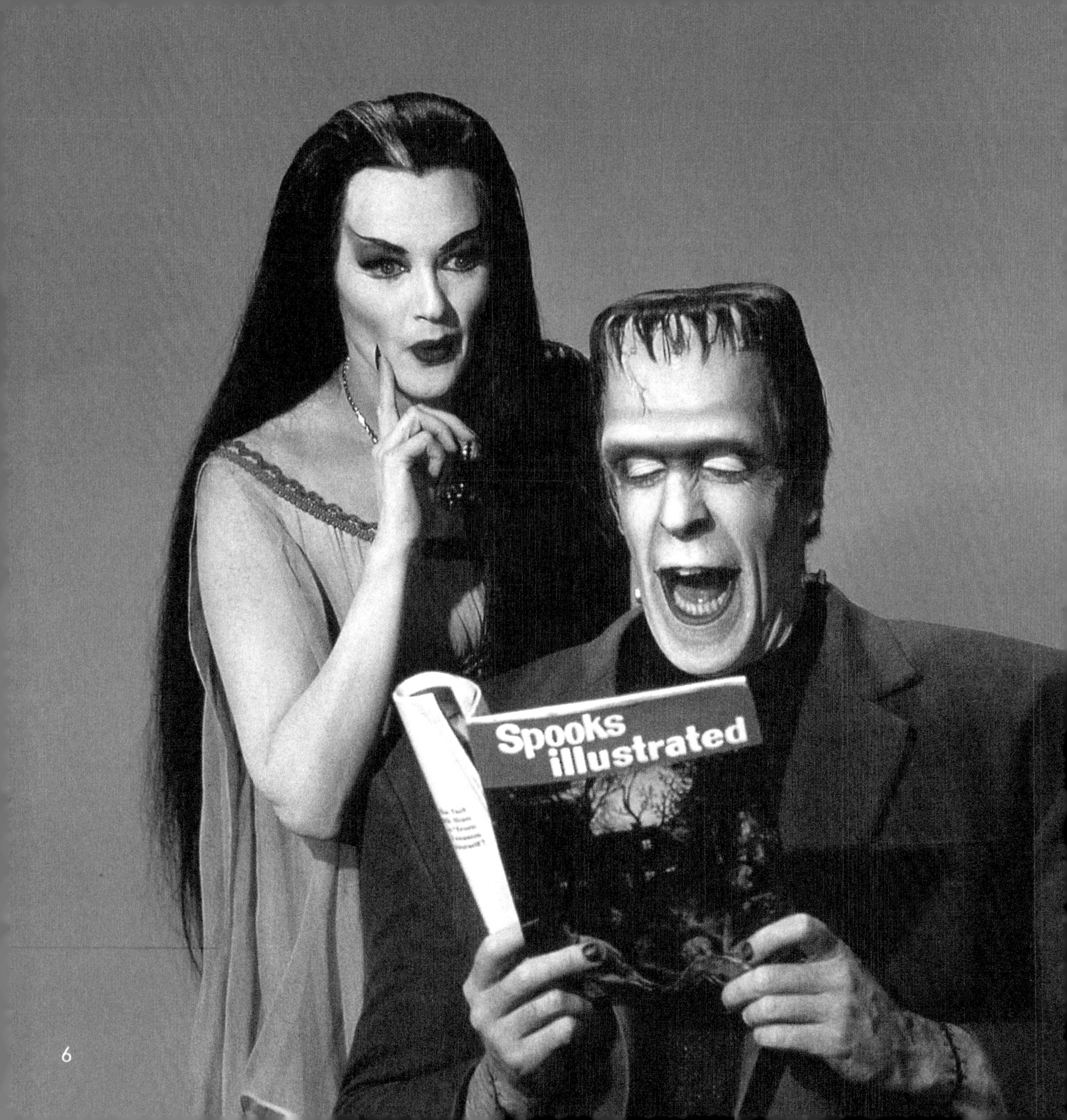
Spooks illustrated

CONTENTS

Hello, Munster Fans!

Congratulations on owning an extremely special publication. This Munster Memories "Coffin" table book is a tribute to you, the fans. I'm Butch Patrick and I had the unbelievable good fortune to play Edward Wolfgang Munster, or "Eddie" as my character is known to the world. Although I acted in several other series and numerous other TV and movie roles, this job will always be what I'll be remembered for. It's been 50 years, and fans still enjoy seeing rerun after rerun on TV, on the DVDs, Netflix, and the internet. This book serves two purposes. First and foremost, to share with you some of the thousands of stories and memories fans have told me, complete with my personal commentary. Second, to bring some never before published facts and pictures to the public. I never get tired of meeting the families who either grew up watching us in the original 1964 to 1966 version, or the new generation that is enjoying it for the first time with their parents or grandparents. Not many shows can entertain all ages and backgrounds like The Munsters. Several factors were present to accomplish this rare feat. First, the writing for the cast was top-notch. Speaking of the actors, Fred Gwynne and Al Lewis were comic geniuses.

The original Goth beauty Lily Munster was the stunningly beautiful Yvonne DeCarlo, whose movie star status gave the show star power. A beautiful cousin who didn't feel pretty was a comic twist which both actresses who portrayed Marilyn Munster reveled in. And the only child Eddie, ME, was a role to die for. Add in the funniest guest stars in Hollywood, custom cars by George Barris, and the best makeup team in the business. The Westmores are legendary to this day. Add special effects and set design by the best Universal Studios had to offer. The monster studio put together a stellar group of professionals to ensure a show the likes of which had never before been seen. The producers had previously done Amos 'n' Andy as well as Leave It To Beaver, and Joe and Bob knew they had something special. This book will take you behind the scenes, with testimonials from key players who actually worked on the show. The fans' input is the backbone of this project. I just put the pieces together and asked a few friends to share their memories. Hope you enjoy it as much as we loved making it.

Butch Patrick

The Munster house on 1313 Mockingbird Lane.

A BRIEF HISTORY OF
THE MUNSTERS

BY RICHARD MAURIZIO

1964 was one of the most interesting and imaginative years for television, with the introduction of some of the most creative and unique shows of all time. Some of these shows have continued in syndication to this day, and are enjoyed by new generation after new generation. These shows include *Johnny Quest*, *The Addams Family*, *Gilligan's Island*, *The Man From U.N.C.L.E.*, *Bewitched*, *Gomer Pyle U.S.M.C.*, *Voyage to the Bottom of the Sea*, and *Underdog*.

The Universal monsters had been enjoying renewed interest due to television syndication. Universal recognized this and decided to develop a television show using these archetypes, and originally envisioned a cartoon series until it was decided to use live actors.

The writing team of Alan Burns and Chris Hayward, the writers of *Rocky and Bullwinkle*, made a presentation very similar to an idea originally suggested by animator Bob Clampett. The job was then assigned to Norm Liebman and Ed Hass to write the pilot. The production team of Bob Mosher and Joe Connely of Revue Productions had completed the hit show *Leave It To Beaver* and were brought on to produce a sixteen-minute pilot. Fred Gwynne and Al Lewis, both of *Car 54, Where Are You?*, were brought on to play the comical team of the series. Gwynne was to play Herman Munster, a seven-foot tall Frankenstein. Lewis was to portray Grandpa Munster, also known as Count Dracula.

Herman Munster in "Herman the Rookie."

Al Lewis and Fred Gwynne.

The original pilot was shot on Alfred Hitchcock's *Psycho* set and was filmed in color. Actress Joan Marshall played Phoebe, the original name for Herman's wife, and Happy Derman was Eddie, their son. Joan Marshall was a character actor that appeared in many television shows, and Happy (Nate) Derman had appeared on *The Beverly Hillbillies* and *Mister Ed*. There is very little else known about him. In the pilot, " My Fair Munster", The Munsters' niece, played by Beverley Owen, is being driven home by her date. As they approach the steps of the creepy looking house, Marilyn's date is a little perplexed and wonders why her family would live there. Marilyn misplaces her keys and knocks on the door. They hear the sound of footsteps and as the door opens we see Herman Munster for the first time. This would be the first and last time Marilyn's date would see Herman because he bolts out of there and speeds off in his car from fright. Poor Marilyn thinks this is all her fault and she wonders why she always scares off her dates, not realizing the reality that it's her creepy but lovable family

After the original pilot was filmed, it was then presented and sold to CBS. Revue Productions was now changed to Kayro-Vue, named after Mosher's and Connely's wives. The network asked for some changes, such as replacing Joan Marshall with movie screen star Yvonne DeCarlo and replacing Happy Derman with well-known child actor Butch Patrick.

13

Beverley Owen with Al Lewis and Butch Patrick.

14

Left: *The cast in place.*
Bottom: *Director Norm Abbot with Gwynne and DeCarlo.*

Butch Patrick (who played Eddie Munster on the show) describes the original thirteen episodes as being about Marilyn and why she couldn't find love and get married, not realizing her family were monsters who scared off any potential suitors. Marilyn eventually became a secondary character and was given fewer lines as the show progressed. He also stated the many times he went back and forth with Al Lewis about this. Lewis always felt the show was about Herman and Grandpa.

During the first season of the show there were some adjustments. Looking at the original episodes, there were constant changes in the makeup. All the actors went through hours of makeup except for Beverley Owen, who was actually a brunette and just had to put on a blonde wig. One example was the nose on Grandpa. In the first few episodes, Al Lewis had a fake nose put on him. It was later decided to eliminate the nose. Fred Gwynne had a lot of trouble with the makeup and

Doctor Dudley, the family doctor, as played by Paul Lynde.
Doctor Dudley was also portrayed by Dom DeLuise.

Top: Jerry Parris, one of the directors on The Munsters, played Jerry the dentist on the Dick Van Dyke Show.

Left: Richard Deacon, who played Mel on the Dick Van Dyke show, appeared as a guest star. Dick Van Dyke himself stopped by for a few photos.

Beverley Owen left the show after thirteen episodes.

the foam padding for his character. Gwynne was said to have developed severe back problems from wearing the padding and headpiece. In some of the episodes, you can notice that Herman's head would be different sizes and the style of makeup would change. In some episodes his face looked thin, and as the series progressed Herman began to look a little less gaunt and less frightening.

Towards the later half of the first season and into the second, the show focused more on Herman, Grandpa and Lily. The character of Herman changed a bit. He became less "by the book" and more childish in nature and a bit naïve at times. Herman and Grandpa would get into some situation or predicament and Lily called the shots. The show encountered another problem in its first season. Beverley Owen asked to be let out of her contract after thirteen episodes, and was replaced by Pat Priest. Priest was the same size as Owen and looked similar. Most viewers didn't notice any difference in the replacement of Marilyn. With the casting change, the opening credits had to be re-shot. This time Herman was shown coming up through the stairs first, given that Fred Gwynne is the first name in the opening credits. The rest of the credits were similar, still spoofing the opening of *The Donna Reed Show*.

In the second season of the show, the credits open with Herman crashing through the front door, looking a bit on the confused side in keeping with his character. The rest of the cast walk through the giant hole that Herman made. Grandpa tries to fit a shovel through the door, with Eddie carrying a large baseball bat. The opening of the theme changed a bit, with a guitar now playing the rhythm instead of a trumpet.

During the original run of the show, the Munsters became a household name. Universal cashed in on this by adding the Munster House to their tram tour. Michael Westmore would also give a makeup demonstration. At times the show would be shooting and the actors would meet with the fans. There was even a staged Lab with Herman or the Frankenstein monster on the table.

Yvonne DeCarlo prepares before a take.

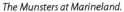
The Munsters at Marineland.

They would also make guest appearances on various TV shows, including *The Danny Kaye Show*, and Gwynne and Lewis appeared in the 1965 Macy's Thanksgiving Day parade. There was even a special called *Marineland Carnival* where the Munsters go to Marineland to find a new pet for Eddie.

So why was *The Munsters* cancelled during its peak? The scripts became weaker, and the advent of color TV made the expense to film the show too costly. *The Munsters* ran for two years and 70 episodes. However, the Munsters were not dead yet. Universal decided to produce a theatrical movie based on the show. *Munster, Go*

Home! was released in 1966. In the movie, the Munsters inherit an English manor and its fortune. They set sail for England, but little do they know they have relatives there, set out to kill Herman. The show reunited the cast, except for Pat Priest, who learned she was to be replaced by contract actor Debbie Watson. Lewis and Gwynne went to the producers to have her on the movie but did not prevail. After the movie, *The Munsters* gained a revival in syndication. Universal wanted to produce a cartoon show, so they went to Fred Calvert Productions, which produced a one-hour special, The Mini-Munsters.

Left: Theatrical poster for Munster, Go Home!
Top: Eddie and Woof Woof in a scene from Munster, Go Home!

Munster, Go Home! Fred, Yvonne, and Debbie Watson as Marilyn with Terry Thomas and Hermione Gingold
as the relatives out to kill Herman.

Top: *International promotion art for Munster, Go Home!*
Right: *Scenes from Munster, Go Home!*

Left: Herman on a lab table at Universal.
Top: Al Lewis greets visitors.

The Mini-Munsters was broadcast as part of the Saturday Superstar movie line-up on ABC. In the show, Eddie was a teenager and, along with his cousins Igor and Lucretia, forms a band. Even Al Lewis returned as the voice of Grandpa.

In 1981, not giving up on their first family of fright, Universal reunited the core three in *The Munsters' Revenge*. Universal was hoping this would lead to a new series, but it did not do well in the ratings. *The Munsters' Revenge* is highly criticized by fans, but there is one classic scene where Herman and Grandpa are disguised as waitresses.

In 1995, Universal debuted *Here Come The Munsters*, produced by John Landis. The film starred Edward Herman as Herman, Veronica Hamel as Lily, and Robert Morse as Grandpa. The film would include a cameo by the original cast and the very last

Left: The Munsters' Revenge reunited Fred Gwynne, Al Lewis and Yvonne DeCarlo in their iconic roles.
Right: The Cast from The Munsters Today - John Schuck, Lee Meriwether and Howard Morton.

appearance together by the original cast.

After *The Munsters*, Fred Gwynne continued to act (mostly on Broadway) but was typecast as the lovable Herman. He concentrated on his passion for art and wrote and illustrated several children's books. In the 1980s, his career in films began to take off again after the films *My Cousin Vinny* and *Pet Sematary*. This led him to do voiceovers in commercials until his death in 1993.

Lewis continued in acting and opened a restaurant in New York City called Grampa's Bella Gente. He continued to use the Grandpa icon and did a series of spots

for TBS called Super Scary Saturday. There was also a skit where Butch Patrick and Pat Priest were involved in playing very familiar roles. He was involved in series of campaigns for McDonald's with other TV icons. He also starred in a movie called *My Grandpa Is A Vampire*. He ran for Governor of NY in 1998 and was a frequent guest on *The Howard Stern Show*. He passed away in 2006.

Yvonne DeCarlo continued in movies and Broadway until she suffered a minor stroke and retired to the Motion Picture and Television Hospital in Woodland Hills. She passed away of natural causes in 2007.

Pat Priest continued in movies and co-starred with Elvis Presley in *Easy Come, Easy Go*. She continues to make appearances at collectible shows throughout the US.

Butch Patrick continues acting and appears at collectible shows and car shows. He was in *The Phantom Tollbooth* and starred in Syd and Marty Kroft's *Lidsville*.

There have been various incarnations of the Munsters, including *Munsters Today* (1988-1991), a series with new actors; *The Munsters' Revenge* (1995); *The Munsters' Scary Little Christmas* (1996); and most recently, a total revamp of The Munsters. But it's the original 70 episodes that are held the closest to every Munster fan's heart.

THE FAMILY ON
1313 MOCKINGBIRD LANE

HERMAN MUNSTER

If you knock on the door of the Munster house and are greeted by a 7ft tall giant…you would have the honor of meeting Herman Munster. There's no need to run away, because this enormous creature, created by Dr. Frankenstein, is a good-natured soul.

Herman is 150 years old, and was built in Germany. He went to college, in six different parts, at the Heidelberg School. After the turn of the century, Herman left Germany. Rumor has it, there were villagers and torches involved. He then arrived in England, where he was taken in by the Noble family of Munster (Munster, Go Home!), hence given the name Herman Munster, also known as the 5th Earl of Shroudshire.

Herman eventually decided to leave Great Britain (rumor has it, there were villagers and torches involved) and ended up in Transylvania. He was not aware at that time that there he would find his true love, Lily.

It was love at first fright for the both of them, so they decided to get married and left across the ocean for America (rumor has it, villagers and torches were involved). They brought along Lily's reluctant father, and moved into an old mansion on 1313 Mockingbird Lane, in a small suburb called Mockingbird Heights, and made it their home.

During the 1940s, America was at war; Herman wanted to do his part and enlisted in the Army. Herman said that when he was in the Army in a foxhole, the enemy would look at him and run. So would the guys on his side.

After he returned from the Army, Herman and Lily took in Lily's niece, Marilyn, and later had a son, who they named Eddie. Herman works at a funeral home in Mockingbird Heights called Gateman, Goodbury and Graves. Mr. Gateman, his boss, hired Herman as a "nail boy" and considered him to be an odd, but loyal employee.

GRANDPA MUNSTER

Downstairs, in the basement of the Munster's house, stands a laboratory with beakers, test tubes, potions, switches, and a bat named Igor. This is the laboratory of Grandpa Munster, also known as Count Dracula, a cranky old vampire and mad scientist.

His ideas are always used for good, but sometimes go wrong, even accidentally turning a little bratty boy into a monkey. Grandpa's inventions or formulas have included an enlarging machine that could make anything bigger and a 'nothing muffin' that once eaten turns something into nothing including Herman's singing voice, and a pill that turns water into gasoline.

He is the oldest member of the family, born in 1367, and loves to reminisce about his old friends that include Richard the Lionheart, Nero, and even Jack the Ripper. He's a bit sarcastic stating his opinions, while sitting in his favorite electric chair, and loves a good cigar and would at times blow smoke out of his ears. Grandpa also loves women so much that he's been married 167 times and still hears from them.

Grandpa can change into a bat or a wolf, which has caused him to get into difficult situations. As a bat, he got chased out of a college dorm by a group of students, and as a wolf he ended up in the pound.

Grandpa loves his family, but has a love-hate relationship with his son-in-law, Herman, and thinks he is too straight, and a bit of a goodie two-shoes. They constantly get on each other's nerves, and when Herman and Grandpa get into trouble they have to deal with his daughter Lily.

Photo by Gene Trindl for TV Guide.

LILY MUNSTER

She has long black hair with a grey streak through it. She wears a long gown and has a bat necklace. She's the Countess of Shroudshire, and named after the flower of death.

Lily was born in 1827, and though you never see her try to drink blood, she is a vampire. She walks out in the day with a heavy cape and hood, and even sleeps like the dead with a flower and her arms crossed.

For years, Lily lived with her father in Transylvania, until Herman swept her off her feet. Herman and Lily tied their nuptials in a mausoleum in the year 1865. "People danced at our wedding that haven't danced in years," she said. After they were married, they had their honeymoon on Devil's Island. She is totally in love with her husband, referring to him at times as "Pussycat".

During the war, Lily served her part by becoming a volunteer airplane spotter. She would sit in the dungeon and watch planes with her crystal ball.

Lily is the one who keeps the family together. She's the one who makes sure the family starts off their day right with a hearty breakfast of pancakes and syrup or oatmeal and then come home to a hearty meal consisting of a roast or a quadruple-legged chicken.

Lily is the voice of reason, but she has a bit of a temper. She's constantly dealing with the antics of her father and her husband. She is a loving, caring creature and very protective of her son, Eddie, and her niece Marilyn.

MARILYN MUNSTER

When you see a young man running down the street with a look of fear on his face, you may have just seen Marilyn's date. He probably just met Marilyn's family and is running in panic.

Marilyn often wonders to herself why she can't keep a man and why she's always the odd one, bearing no resemblance to any of her family. They can't understand why she can't find a nice guy and get married, either. When she does meet a man, they always think it's charitable of him to not be concerned of her looks, or as they put it, her misfortune.

Marilyn is Lily and Herman's niece. Her mother is Lily's sister, and she's lived with Herman and Lily since she was a child. There is no known reason why Marilyn was taken in by Herman and Lily, but she is a great help to her family. Marilyn is always helping her aunt around the household and looks at their odd lifestyle as normal. She also helps her aunt take care of the youngest member, Eddie.

EDWARD WOLFGANG MUNSTER

If you hear howling coming out of the Munster house at night…that may be the youngest member of the family howling at the moon. This little boy in a fauntleroy suit, with pointed ears, fangs, and a widow's peak, is Eddie, proud son of Herman and Lily, and also a werewolf.

He is a playful, but sometimes mischievous child, who likes to enter the kitchen through the cabinet, and sleeps in a chest of drawers. He looks up to his parents and grandfather, especially his father. He loves to boast about his dad and his accomplishments. This sometimes gets Herman into difficult situations. One time, Eddie got his dad into a drag race, causing them to temporarily lose the family car. Eddie also carries a huge baseball bat and loves to get into large mouse traps.

His two favorite things are his doll Woof Woof, which resembles a 1940s movie Werewolf, and his pet, Spot, who lives under the stairs.

A father and son moment.

ABOUT MY FAMILY
BY BUTCH PATRICK

The cast for the first thirteen episodes with Beverley Owen.

First off is Fred Gwynne, the level-headed one in the family. This was definitely HIS show. No one could replace him as Herman Munster. He worked tirelessly and set a standard for all of us. A favorite memory was his pranks on the prop men who would build models and fragile works only to have Fred destroy them in the shot. They usually built two, knowing there was a good chance he would break one in rehearsal. MY personal memory was how he taught me to be a hipster in the episode 'The Musician'. Talking cool wasn't really what an 11 year old was all about. Fun stuff for sure.

Second, Yvonne DeCarlo - the coolest TV mom EVER, in my opinion. Her look and beauty balanced out the monster of Frankenstein and Dracula perfectly. She was a REAL movie star and came to TV before it was commonplace. The memory I remember most was how good she was at doing comedy. That, and playing my protector in ZOMBO was priceless. Good woman who I became close to in her later years. I loved it when she said I was "very" talented, and referred to me as her TV baby.

Third, Al Lewis. Hmmmm, so many memories to pick from. I'll use two. First, from the show. Al loved sports and when time permitted he would go outside and toss a frisbee or a baseball with me. It may not sound like much, but when you're the only kid on an entire studio lot, believe me, it's an important few minutes. Second was the opening of his restaurant. I was honored that he included me in such a BIG event in his life. Had a wonderful time and didn't know at the time of the connected ownership of Grampa's Restaurant.

33

The cast with Pat Priest.

Fourth, the Marilyns. First up is Beverley Owen. VaVaVooom. I had SUCH a crush on Bev!!! She left the show after 3 months, but before she did she made a young man very happy. She actually drove down to my house like 20 miles away, picked me up and drove up to Grauman's Chinese Theater to see Mary Poppins. I was in the clouds. This was a huge movie release and I was with my dream girl. Emphasis on the dream. I like to say that was my first date!

Pat Priest has become a dear friend, and my best memory of her comes as an adult after the show. Pat had invited me up to Idaho, and I finally took her up on it. I was concerned that dropping in on such short notice might be a bad idea. What if she wasn't doing so well? Maybe she had no room for us and was being nice. Well, no need to worry about the unfortunate one on the show. As we pulled up to this beautiful home in Hailey, Idaho my concerns vanished. As I was to learn, her neighbors were Bruce and Demi, and I believe a CEO or some high ranking exec of Bank of America was on the other side. Pat was the unofficial Mayor of Hailey and Sun Valley in general. The stories she shared were hysterical. You see, Pat did well in real estate in a little city called Beverly Hills.

There were also different directors who were so important to the quality of the episodes, and writers who went on to greatness as well. Just top notch talent across the board was our blessing.

AN INTERVIEW WITH A VAMPIRE

BY RICHARD MAURIZIO

This interview with Al Lewis was originally conducted in 1992 at Grampa's restaurant in New York City.

Question: To start, we would like to ask you about yourself…your career.

AL LEWIS: I'll talk to you about anything…are you depressed? Do you love your mother?…anything (laughter). Start off with the first intelligent question.

Q: According to your biography, before you went into acting, you held various positions. What types of jobs did you do?

LEWIS: Well, I've been a performer since 1922. I worked at the circus, I worked at the carnival, burlesque…I did eighteen years of radio, Broadway, off-Broadway, movies and television. Then, when you're out of work, you still have to eat and pay rent.

Q: Of course.

LEWIS: So, I was a plumber's helper, worked on the docks, was a store detective, was a toy salesman…I had a million jobs (laughter).

Q: You also taught school?

LEWIS: Yeah.

Q: What did you teach?

LEWIS: Well, I received a PHD in Psychology from Columbia. I was a child psychologist.

Q: And from that you wrote children's books?

LEWIS: Yeah. I have written more than have been published (laughter), but four have been published.

Photos by Alexander Maurizio.

Q: What were they?

LEWIS: "How to" books – How to Take a Train Ride, How to Go with Mother to the Market…they were written on the children's level.

Q: When were they published?

LEWIS: In the 1960s.

Q: Would you say you're a person who likes to do different things and then go on to something else?

LEWIS: Well, I've done different things to remain a performer. I've never sat. I drifted from one form of entertainment to another. You do what you can to stay alive.

Q: What got you into acting?

LEWIS: I don't know what got me actually into acting. I started out in the circus. I don't know if you call that acting. I call myself a performer. I got into radio at WGN in Chicago, then went to WLW, and then from there I came to New York and was in big time radio. That's when there only was radio – there was no television, you know. They saw I could read lines and be effective, so they said, "Okay, you're an actor in radio," so from acting in radio, I went to television, films, and Broadway. It wasn't like a kind of choice of mind; I just drifted from one to the other. I fit in.

Q: And to performing on live television…

LEWIS: It was a long time back. Nobody does live television history today. It was very challenging (and) I loved it. Doing live television is the same thing as doing a Broadway show. As the curtain goes up and the overture starts, there's no stopping and starting. That's it.

Fred Gwynne with Al Lewis, always seen with a cigar. Also notice the variation in Gwynne's makeup on Herman.

Anything I've ever done, short time or long time, I have a great time because, as I say, I bring it with me. I work hard. I give 122% and I have fun. If I'm not having fun, I quit – oh, I've quit jobs! What have I lost? I haven't lost a life or career. I'll get another job, no big deal.

Q: Is Car 54 where you met Fred Gwynne?

LEWIS: No, I knew him from around. In those years, actors were making rounds, so Fred was a New York actor. We would run into each other for coffee, or I'd see him on the street, so I knew him from around town.

Q: He also designed the logo for your restaurant?

LEWIS: He drew it. He was a Fine Arts major at Harvard. He's a great sculptor (and) a fine artist.

Q: He's also done children's books.

LEWIS: Oh! He's done sixteen books, which he both writes and illustrates. He's a great artist.

Lewis takes a bite out of Frank (Fair Deal Dan) Gorshin on the set.

The cast with Beverley Owen.

Q: Let's move on to The Munsters. How did you get the part of Grandpa?

LEWIS: I was home. The phone rang (and) a gentleman by the name of Jerry Henshaw called. He said he was in charge of new projects at Universal and asked me if I would be interested in doing a pilot, so I told him I didn't know and I asked him to send me a script. About, four days later, I flew out to California and we did the presentation. The presentation ran about twelve minutes and it showed the family. Fred was there. There was another lady, Joan Marshall, it wasn't Yvonne DeCarlo, and then there was another boy…Happy Derman, and Beverly Owen who

was a contract player. There was a little scene and then it shifted to the lab. I ad-libbed about a six or seven minute scene and that was the whole thing.

Q: What was the actual shooting schedule like?

LEWIS: We would get the script on Friday, and look it over on the weekend, come in and read the script for timing for what they think works and doesn't work. Monday we would come in for an hour and a half and then we went home. They sent us different

Al Lewis with Richard Maurizio.

colored pages for where they would make cuts or add (material). Tuesday we walked it around on the set, not the whole cast, just the principles for the director of Photography, and Wednesday, Thursday and Friday we shot it.

Q: Going into the makeup on the series, how long did it take?

LEWIS: Two hours…I would come in at 6 a.m. My makeup man was one of the most famous names in makeup- Perc Westmore. I was in at 6 a.m. and had to be ready by 8 a.m.

Q: Did you have any involvement in the scripts?

LEWIS: Involvement in the sense that Fred and I would complain, or yell or make suggestions, which were generally thrown into the toilet. The telephone booth in the casket was our idea. The family pet, Spot, was our idea. A matter of fact, Fred designed the Dragon…the head…then the prop department would make it. That's about it, I would say.

Q: Were you involved in the creation of Grandpa?

LEWIS: Oh, sure.

Q: I have read that you developed the walk and his mannerisms.

LEWIS: Well, in a way I was fortunate. Although it would not have affected me in any way because I live by the philosophy: if they give you ruled paper, write the other way. But, in a sense, I didn't have to do that because nobody could say, "No, wait a minute, You can't do that. This is the way it's supposed to be done." There was no precedence for this crazy Dracula-like comic. They can't say, "Do it like Bela Lugosi." In a sense, it was ground-breaking and plus, the way I attack something, I attack it with such discipline and surety. I'm not indefinite. I make choices and I go right with them and that was it – (like) the walk and being heavier. I wore a pregnancy pad to be heavier. Matter of fact, they stole the character idea for Penguin in Batman.

Fred GWYNNE
and
Al LEWIS
STARS OF
The CBS-TV series
'The MUNSTERS"

Al Lewis and Fred Gwynne at
the Macy's Thanksgiving Day Parade.

Fred Gwynne and Al Lewis taking a break in the makeup room.

Q: Did the censors have anything to say about the show?

LEWIS: First of all, they don't use the phrase in television. They call them the "continuity man." If they did (have anything to say) we wouldn't hear about it. That's number one, but even though rumors trickled down, I can't predict what human beings think, but I don't know what would offend anybody in that show. No, I never heard of it.

Q: Going from the first year to the second year of the show, did you see any changes?

LEWIS: Ours happened to be what is called, a very heavy show, "Heavy" meaning a lot of special effects. Special effects cost money, reason being is it's a lot of time to set them up while everyone else is sitting around and then in the filming, if it doesn't work, you have to sit around again a lot of the time while they set it up again. So, when the show had the immediate success it did, this will happen in all of television. But in ours, even more so in the first two, three shows if it catches on…everything goes including the bathtub. After that, it gets skimpy.

Q: Do you have any favorite episodes?

LEWIS: I've never seen it. I've never seen anything I ever did.

Q: Really? That's interesting.

LEWIS: I watch very little television. I mean, when people say, "I remember you did this." I kind of recall in my mind's eye, but I've never physically seen the show.

Q: Why do you think the show was canceled when it was high in the ratings?

Grampa's Super Silly Scaries and a menu to Grampa's Restaurant.

LEWIS: I absolutely have no idea. You have to understand that a performer is, in spite of what quote unquote stars think (not realizing stars are only in the heavens), they're not even informed. What happens is Friday you're told, "Don't come in Monday!" (laughter). I have absolutely no idea...I would guess the accounting department said, "We threw the numbers into the mainframe computer we have in the basement and it tells us that we can make more money syndicating it rather than just keep making new shows." In this particular case, it proved that to them, because it's now running twenty-eight years in syndication in forty-four countries in the world still. Twenty-eight years after I finished doing it and they get paid for that, so they were right.

Q: After the series, you did Munster, Go Home! and...

LEWIS: The history of The Munsters is, we did a one-hour Easter show in Marineland, we did Munster,Go Home! in-between the first and second year, and then years after, we did Munsters' Revenge. That's the history of the extra-curricular Munsters. As a matter of fact, Fred and I toured the New York City theaters with the picture (Munster, Go Home!).

Q: What in your opinion makes for good comedy?

LEWIS: It makes you laugh. I'm not philosophical enough. I can make people laugh, but if it has to be a one-page essay on why people laugh, I have no idea.

Q: Well, we would like to thank you for your time for this interview.

LEWIS: Thank you. It was my pleasure.

ZOMBO!

ZOMBO, one of the classic episodes from the second season. ZOMBO was played by Louis Nye.

LEFT: *Behind the scenes during the filming of Zombo.*

TOP: *A scene from the episode Zombo.*

LILY MUNSTER
THE ORIGINAL GOTH MOM

BY KRISTINA KREEP PIERCE

Lily Munster has influenced me as a wife and mother. Funny thing is, I had just been in the hospital the night before in early labor with my second daughter, who my first daughter has nicknamed Lily (short for Lydia). What timing!

I first started watching The Munsters as a child through the reruns of shows, TV movies, and even the reboot movies. It was easy to be bewitched by Lily. She was the first matriarch of the Munster family, inviting even with her gothic style, and drop dead gorgeous! She has influenced everything from my personal style of raven black hair, forever red lips and spooky dresses, to the way I run my home. I often refer to my family as modern day Munsters, not only because our **dynamic is very** much that of Herman and Lily. Years of weekly Munsters watching will do that! I'd be lying if I said I didn't have WWLD (what would Lily do?) moments. She's really everything I think a woman should be. She was a loving mom, like myself, and her appearance didn't have any effect on that! She always stood behind Herman, even when she was secretly making things work, and she was endlessly devoted.

From the outside, I am what most would consider a goth mom. I even have Lily and Herman tattooed on my arm, so my love for the Munsters is literally worn on my sleeve! This brands me as different and weird. Like Lily, I get lots of looks and judgement, but that has never stopped me! My family definitely lives a spooky lifestyle but the truth is, like the Munsters, we are extremely traditional. Once you get past the spooky image, you see I'm a loving, supportive mom and wife. Ok, maybe I have more bats. One can never have too many bats! If anything, I believe being an "alternative" mother will only give my kids an open mind. They don't see tattoos, hair color, or style. They see people. And even being the odd woman out in the group of moms at ballet class, my daughter still holds my hand proudly. Handling every situation with confidence and always being a class act, despite how the outside world views you, is something I absolutely took from Lily Munster. But if you mess with my pussycat (aka husband) or children, that fiery temper will come out!

MICHAEL WESTMORE

I had just finished my Makeup Apprenticeship at Universal Studios in 1964, when "The Munsters" were born. Everyone at the Studio was so excited to resurrect Universal's Famous Monster characters from the 30s and 40s into an upbeat comedy. There was no one more excited than my Uncle Bud, who was the Makeup Supervisor for Universal. Ahead of filming, the makeup for each character was well designed and creatively thought out. The makeup artists hired by my Uncle Bud to apply their skill were some of Hollywood's best. My Uncle Perc, the master, took care of Grandpa Munster; Karl Silvera, Herman; Abe Haberman; Lilly, and the new kid on the block, me, was assigned to Eddie and Marilyn (Pat Priest). Every morning, all of us applied the individual facial makeup and some latex appliances, like Eddie's ears and Herman's head, so hairstyling and wardrobe would complete the Munster image. With Eddie, following a coat of pale facial makeup, I had to adhere (with glue) a small triangle piece of hair to give him the prominent widow's peak, which is a signature of the beasts in many Vampire movies. Finally, I glued on a pair of bushy eyebrows. Butch had naturally prominent teeth, so it wasn't necessary to make him a pair of Vampire fangs. After everyone finished, Uncle Perc, Karl, and Abe would proceed to the filming stage to take personal care of their performers. I would climb the stairway outside the makeup department, up to the old makeup lab where most of Universal's rubber aliens and monsters hung out. It was an old, dusty room, filled with plaster faces that were used in the past to create special makeup. It looked a lot like the inside of the Munster house…cobwebs and all. My daily assignment was to create a new pair of pointed latex ears for Butch, and a new flat headpiece and neck bolts for Herman. And that is how I spent most of my time for the run of the Munster series.

In show business, the established bonds of friendship never seem to break. From the days that Butch would climb up into my large hydraulic makeup chair, right up to the present where we meet at a SyFy or Monster Convention, it all seems like yesterday. Butch revealed to me in later years that he really looked up to me. I respected him as an intelligent

Recent photo of Michael Westmore from Butch's cell phone.

and well-mannered child; he was fun to be around. From his point of view, I was tanned from weekly sailing, drove a Jaguar, wore an Ascot to work, and was a bachelor until 1965 at least, when I met the most beautiful woman in the world. Yeah, Butch… I can see your point.

Butch's little werewolf doll Woof-Woof was created in our special makeup lab at the top of the stairs. The cloth body was constructed in the Wardrobe Department, supervised by the famous Designer Edith Head.

Woof-Woof's head and hands came to life in front of an old Creature from the Black Lagoon suit that hung in a dusty corner. All three pieces were sculpted in clay by either Chris Muller, who had previously sculpted the Lagoon Creature, or John Chambers, who later won an Academy Award for The Planet of the Apes. Both of these artists were employed by my Uncle Bud at that time, for other projects. I don't remember which one was responsible, but they were both geniuses. After the Studio approved the sculptures, they were molded. The parts were constructed out of latex, painted, hair was glued to Woof's head and a beard onto his face. Upon completion, the head and hands were attached to the body and Woof-Woof was ready to go to work. Silly me, at the time the doll was considered just a "Prop". With a little foresight I could have had an original Woof-Woof.

I was involved with the Universal tours from DAY 1 in 1963. It was a very small, micro mini version of what consumes acres of land and amusements today.

There were 2 trams to shuttle the 1000 tourists per week and 4 tour guides that alternated between rides through the Universal lot. My part started small, as I would give a makeup demonstration to a full tram of people several times a day. It all grew very fast, as more trams and tour guides were added. I eventually would give a demonstration 10 times a day. An Edith Head fashion show was designed to precede the makeup demonstration, and this is where I met my beautiful wife Marion, who was a model for Edith. Excitement like this is what I would share with Butch in our morning makeup sessions and he would tell me of his adventures.

At that time in 1964, "The Munsters" was just another, but popular, television show of the 60s. Reruns and the fans would not let it die, and it is pure escapism entertainment. The writing was fun, and the characters were fun, including the guest stars. No matter how it was resurrected with other performers, in my opinion, the television audience and fans of today still cherish and faithfully remember the original characters that established it all. 50 years later, little Butch Patrick is and always will be THE Eddie Munster.

The old-school monsters scared the be-Jesus out of millions of moviegoers for decades. With the Munsters format, the audience could sit back and enjoy the antics and situations of a monster world now full of humor. Adults and children of all ages could go to sleep without having to check under the bed or having a nightmare. Laughter and little Eddie made everything all right.

-*Michael Westmore*

Butch and Michael Westmore.

Michael Westmore with an Oscar.

STAR WEEKLY

AUGUST 27, 1966   20 CENTS

SCHOOL'S IN
With a new schoolmarm
and
A new wardrobe for the teens

YVONNE DE CARLO
VANCOUVER'S CO...

TV prevue   APRIL 25-MAY 1
● Free every Sunday with your Chicago Sun-Times

THE MUNSTERS

Listings—Mar. 14-Mar. 20

AY, MARCH 14, 1965

PAT PRIEST . . GLAMOR AMONG THE

50

AN INTERVIEW WITH
PAT PRIEST

Pat Priest has been acting since childhood. She has been in dozens of TV commercials and TV shows including Bewitched, My Favorite Martian, The Lucy Show and Mission Impossible. She also had a notable recurring role on The Mary Tyler Moore Show playing Betty White's unappreciated younger sister. But the role she is best known for playing is the odd one in the family, Marilyn Munster.

Q: How did you get the role for Marilyn?

Pat Priest: Well, the producers for the show were looking for a replacement. Beverley Owen, who played Marilyn in the first thirteen episodes, wanted to leave the show to move to New York and get married. My agent got me a test on the last day of testing. I was one of five girls auditioning for the role. I tested on Wednesday and Thursday and they told me I got the part. On Friday I signed the contract and Monday I was on the set.

Q: Did you ever meet Beverly Owen, the first Marilyn?

PP: To this day I have never met her. I would love to meet her and talk to her. We share a common experience together.

It's funny, I go to these collectors shows and at times, people would hand me a picture of her to sign. So, I nicely tell them 'I can't sign this because this isn't a photo of me". (Laughter)

Q: Had you seen the show before ?

PP: No, I heard about it but I never did see it. I think it was better that way because I didn't see how Beverley portrayed her and I could make the character my own.

Q: What was a average day on the set like?

PP: I was at the studio around 6 AM and left around 7 PM. On Monday we would have a read through, on Tuesday we had our rehersal and Wednesday to Friday we would film the episode. I lived forty miles from the studio so there would be long nights.

Q: Do you have any favorite episodes?

PP: The ones where I had more than two lines. (Laughter) I liked the episodes where I would bring a boyfriend home and they would see the family and run away.

Q: So what was your favorite Munster memory?

PP: My favorite Munster memory is how Al and Fred made me laugh. I was always around them. We would take our break from filming and go into the commissary. People would ask me how I could sit there and eat while they were in makeup. We would talk about our families and lives.They were constantly joking around. When Al was alive I would see him at shows and he would still pull jokes on me.

Q: Did you stay in touch with the cast after the show?

PP: I didn't see Uncle Herman after the show. I only saw Aunt Lily once. I reunited with Butch when we started doing the shows together. Butch did visit me here in Idaho where I live.

Q: After The Munsters, what did you do?

PP: I went back and did some television. I did a movie with Elvis Presley called *Easy Come, Easy Go!* After I finished doing the movie with Elvis, he had an Eldorado Cadillac he wanted to sell. I had the key chain with the initials E.P. on it. I ended up trading in the car. I joke to myself that was one of my retirement plans. (laughter). I did a horror movie with Bruce Dern and Casey Kasem called *The Incredible 2-Headed Transplant.*

Q: Why do you think The Munsters are still appealing after 50 years?

PP: I'm amazed at how many times people have come up to me and told me the show was a good wholesome show and non-violent. The show has morals to it and we were a family that functioned. Their families just love it.

Q: Well, thank you for this interview and celebrating 50 years of The Munsters.

MY MUNSTER MEMORY
BY PAT PRIEST

"My favorite Munster memory is how Al and Fred made me laugh. I was always around them. We would take our break from filming and go into the commissary. People would ask me how I could sit there and eat while they were in makeup. We would talk about our families and lives. They were constantly joking around".

REAL RECIPES FROM LILY MUNSTER'S SECRET FAMILY COOKBOOK

BY CHRIS YAMBAR

The following recipes were culled from a massive brittle-paged collection of ancient arcane recipes obtained at an onsite auction many decades ago by oddity hunter and Master Chef Chris Yambar. Although many of the original ingredients and combinations are still universally outlawed and have been known to cause horrific gastronomical side effects (even by European standards), each recipe has been recreated in Chef Yambar's personal test kitchen and has been modified for modern human standards of consumption. The recipe titles have been kept intact and are helpful when told to youngsters and family members who are normally finicky eaters unless the meal has a gross or weird title to arouse their curiosity.

"I'll never forget the night I obtained this collection of family recipes from that creepy old estate," Yambar recalls. "After placing winning bids on some giant work boots, a growling canine doll and some of the strangest Victorian furniture I've ever seen, I was treated to a unique fireworks display. It seems that an auction worker decided to take a smoke break in the basement laboratory of the home without paying attention to the 'Warning: Explosive' signs posted on nearly every flat surface. As bidders scattered and the house burst into colorful explosive flames, the auctioneer shoved the chain-sealed cookbook into my hands and ran down the street in terror. Before driving away, I looked back at the smoking ruins and saw a giant bat circling overhead. Maybe it was the excitement of the moment, but I swear I heard it laughing like an old man as it disappeared into the moonlight."

Here are a few of the recipes found in this amazingly rare monster cookbook:

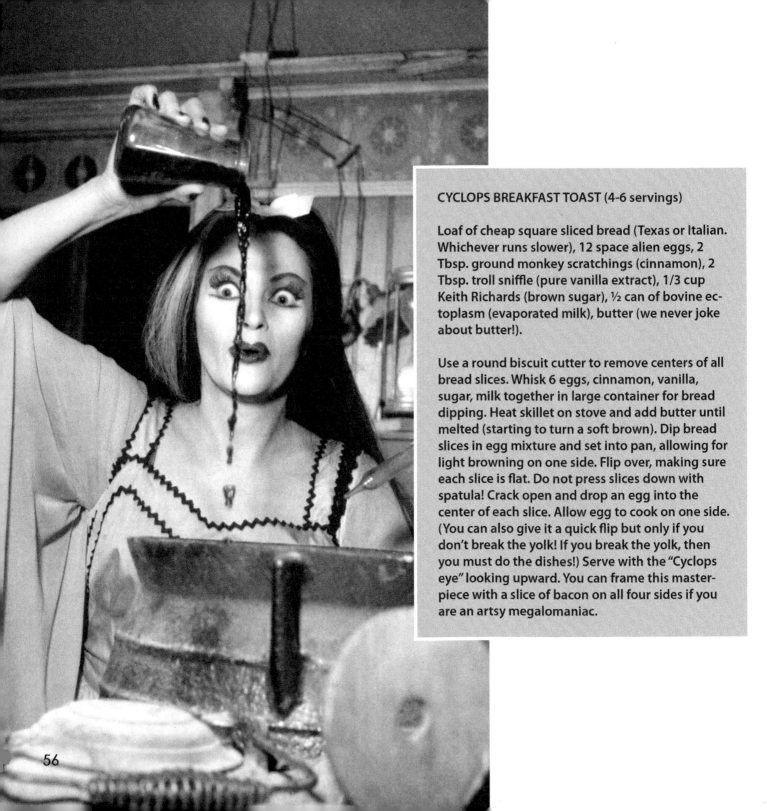

CYCLOPS BREAKFAST TOAST (4-6 servings)

Loaf of cheap square sliced bread (Texas or Italian. Whichever runs slower), 12 space alien eggs, 2 Tbsp. ground monkey scratchings (cinnamon), 2 Tbsp. troll sniffle (pure vanilla extract), 1/3 cup Keith Richards (brown sugar), ½ can of bovine ectoplasm (evaporated milk), butter (we never joke about butter!).

Use a round biscuit cutter to remove centers of all bread slices. Whisk 6 eggs, cinnamon, vanilla, sugar, milk together in large container for bread dipping. Heat skillet on stove and add butter until melted (starting to turn a soft brown). Dip bread slices in egg mixture and set into pan, allowing for light browning on one side. Flip over, making sure each slice is flat. Do not press slices down with spatula! Crack open and drop an egg into the center of each slice. Allow egg to cook on one side. (You can also give it a quick flip but only if you don't break the yolk! If you break the yolk, then you must do the dishes!) Serve with the "Cyclops eye" looking upward. You can frame this masterpiece with a slice of bacon on all four sides if you are an artsy megalomaniac.

IMPOSSIBLE WEREWOLF PIE (6-8 servings)

½ lb. ground beef, ½ lb. ground sausage, 3 owl eggs, ½ t. Dead Sea salt, 1 ½ cups chopped sweet onion, ¼ t. unconsecrated ground black pepper, 1 ½ cups bat milk, 1 cup shredded cheddar cheese, ¾ cup Mummy Dust (Bisquick), small can of Yak blood (tomato puree).

Pre-heat blast furnace to 400 degrees. Grease 10" glass pie plate. Brown beef, sausage and onion and drain grease. Stir in S&P and dump into greased pie plate. Beat milk, Bisquick and eggs in blender until smooth (15 seconds in blender on HI or 1 minute with hand blender or 8 minutes with actual bullwhip). Pour over meat. Administer last rites. Bake 25 minutes. Remove to add puree and shredded cheese to top. Bake additional 5-8 minutes or until knife comes out clean after test stabbing. Cool remains for 5 minutes. Serve. WARNING: It is impossible for real werewolves to resist!

DEVILED DEVILED EGGS (12 servings)

Dozen extra large Voodoo eggs, 2 cans sliced beets, ¼ cup balsamic vinegar, ghost squeeze (mayonnaise), (wasp innards) yellow mustard, (demon tears) hot sauce.

Hard-boil eggs on stove; remove and slide into ice water for shock treatment. (Eggs are hard-boiled when you can spin them on a flat surface. Ice water breaks shell away from inner egg, making it easier to peel.) Send shells to Hell. Place eggs into sealed container. Add beets, juice and vinegar. Put in refrigerator for 2 days to allow them to soak up color and flavor. Remove eggs, cut eggs in half lengthwise. Arrange egg whites on serving plate. Scoop yolks into a separate bowl to pulverize into a smooth spread. Mix in mayonnaise and mustard. (Add as much of each as you like. It's your life.) Spoon mixture into egg whites. Poke pinkie finger into center of each filled egg as you would an ogre's eyeball. Chill. Drop a dot or two of hot sauce into each poke hole right before serving. WARNING: May make butt shake like a snake on a campfire!

EDDIE'S PEANUT BUTTER BACON MUNCH (1 serving)

3 slices of cooked two-headed-pig bacon, 2 slices of bread, an Albino witch's nose (banana), Zombie toe jam (peanut butter), butter.

Place the buttered bread slices into a small heated pan like you would when making a grilled cheese sandwich, buttered side down. Do not stack on top of each other. When each slice is crisp on the "down" side, remove from the pan. Cut banana into long strips and place on top of one uncooked side of bread. Plaster the other bread slice's uncooked side with peanut butter. If you use crunchy peanut butter, then you can pretend you are eating bugs. Add your bacon slices. Fold together, cut into 4 pieces and eat. WARNING: This is the little brother to the sandwich that killed Elvis. Enjoy!

CEMETARY RELISH (Serves us right!)

1 bag of cranberries (washed and dried), 3 goblin apples (washed, peeled, cored), 2 "nothing rhymes with" oranges (peeled, quartered, seeded), 1 more orange with peel on, 1 cup sugar, 1 cup yellow raisins, ½ cup booberries.

Coarsely grind all of the above (except for the sugar, blueberries and yellow raisins) in a food chopper. Put into a large serving bowl and gently stir in booberries, raisins and sugar. Chill until it is time to serve as a side dish at your next monster bash! WARNING: Make sure all of your guests have a Last Will and Testament, because someone is going to kill for the final serving of this! A fitting monument to a meal done well.

ORIENTAL VULTURE NEST SALAD (6-8 servings)

Mix together 3–4 cooked and cubed vulture (chicken) breasts, 1 ½ decapitated and finely chopped lettuce heads, 4 thinly diced green onions with stalks, 1 small package of slivered almonds, 1/2 cup candied peanuts, ¼ cup insulted sunflower seeds.

In a separate bowl, mix together 4 Tbsp. brown sugar, 4 Tbsp. apple cider vinegar, ½ t. unconsecrated ground black pepper, ½ cup of salad oil (truffle or olive).

Blend the 2 mixtures above together at your next coven or church pot luck dinner. IMPORTANT!!!!! MIX IN 1 PACKAGE OF UNCOOKED, CRUNCHED UP RAMEN NOODLES RIGHT BEFORE YOU'RE READY TO SERVE! (Do not add the flavor packet!) WARNING: This is so powerfully delicious that it turns most humans into ravenous pigs on a rampage!

CHRIS YAMBAR is a Pop Art painter, comic creator, children's book author, public speaker and one hell of an excellent cook! He can be reached at: cyambar@hotmail.com. All recipes herein are copyright Chris Yambar 2014. All rights reserved. photo by Jimmy Proctor

FRED GWYNNE: RENAISSANCE MAN

BY RICHARD MAURIZIO

We all loved him as the terminally lovable Herman Munster, but did you know that Fred Gwynne was also an acclaimed musician, sculptor, writer and visual artist?

Fred's father was a successful stockbroker, but his true talent came from his mother, Dorothy Ficken. She was a skilled designer who, in 1901, co-created a popular comic strip and logo character named Sunny Jim for Force cereal. The character was so enduring that his image continued to appear on the cereal box in North America until 1983 and in the United Kingdom until 2013 when production of the brand was retired.

In his youth Fred attended the exclusive prep school Groton and performed in several stage plays. Afterwards, he served as a radioman in the U. S. Navy during World War II. When the war finally ended, Gwynne attended Harvard University, where he studied drawing with portrait artist R. S. Merryman. It was here that his artistic abilities really started to develop. Upon graduation, he worked as a musician, copywriter and professional illustrator.

According to Munsters co-star Butch Patrick, "Throughout his life, Fred would always act, sculpt, write, draw and play music. He was a true renaissance man."

In1958 Gwynne had his first book published. *Best in Show* humorously featured pets and their owners that looked exactly alike. The book was reformatted and later reissued with the title, *Easy to See Why* in 1993.

Following *Best in Show*, his second book, *What's Nude*, was published in 1960. The book contained a series of racy cartoons combined with a photo or group of photos featuring nude women incorporated into each. It was pretty frisky fare for its time.

In 1961, after an appearance on the legendary Phil Silvers Show, Fred was offered the lead role in the TV comedy sitcom "Car 54, Where Are You?" where he played Officer Francis Muldoon. The show quickly became a laugh riot hit and Fred Gwynne was soon a household name.

In the midst of his growing celebrity, Fred made time for his art, and illustrated the book *The Battle of the Frogs and the Mice*. This story, written by author George Martin, was a modern retelling of an ancient Greek fable about an unnecessary war between frogs and mice. Gwynne's hauntingly brilliant drawings made a great impact on those who read the book and really drove home the anti-war theme of its author. Considered by some critics as strong social and political commentary, the book was considered a must-read classic and powerful reflection of its time.

Then came Gwynne's legendary role as television's favorite civilized monster, Herman Munster. "(Fred) brought the character to life. He and Herman were one and the same," states Tony Greco, one of the world's top authorities on the Munsters. "Nobody could have done it better!" "(Fred) was constantly drawing caricatures of people and playing music on the set," added Butch Patrick.

Gwynne even incorporated some of his own art in a Munsters episode, when Herman decided to become a detective and was hired to track someone down. In typical ironic fashion the person he was actually seeking turned out to be none other than…himself! As Herman was drawing the description of his investigation, it was obvious to Grandpa Munster that it was Herman all along. Greco, who owns a variety of Gwynne's original pieces, states that the drawing produced for that episode was "definitely drawn by Fred himself."

After the show was cancelled, Fred continued his acting and took some small roles here and there, and even appeared on Broadway.

The late Al (Grandpa Munster) Lewis was quoted as saying, "Fred was a terriffic actor but he was an incredible artist. That's where his true passion was. I told him to stay with his art."

Drawing Fred Gwynne drew for the episode " Follow That Munster"

Fred returned to his true passion and was inspired by his daughter Madyn to produce a new series of children's books. He decided to incorporate his love for word play, puns and art into playful books such as *The King Who Rained*, *A Chocolate Moose for Dinner* and *A Little Pigeon Toad*.

Gwynne would occasionally illustrate himself into his books. In *A Chocolate Moose for Dinner* he drew himself in a scene where he sat upon a toaster. In *The King Who Rained* he drew himself with a furry mole on his nose.

In *The King Who Rained* the very first pun in the book reads, "Daddy says there was a King who rained for forty years." The illustration shows a King with droplets sprinkling out of him like a cloud while a child stands next to him in his raincoat. Another illustration shows a child with "bear feet" instead of "bare feet."

STORIES TO GO!

The King Who Rained

by FRED GWYNNE

The King Who Rained, the most acclaimed book by Fred Gwynne.

The King Who Rained turned out to be his most popular book in the series and is still being published and enjoyed by readers of all ages. Fred also wrote and illustrated several complete storybooks, including *Pondlarker*, a reworking of *The Princess and the Frog*. The focus of the book is from the frog's point of view and has it's own unique twist to the tale.

His most controversial book was *The Story of Ick*, which was a story about a boy looking for something to play with. Eventually the boy meets Ick, a goopy creature who scoops him up and takes him back to his home in a cave. Ick's parents tell him to put the boy back so that "more boys will grow." Ick obeys and puts the boy back but sadly never finds another to play with ever again. The story gives the impression that, in the future, pollution has evolved and man becomes an endangered species. The book is drawn in a very simple style and with no color. While Gwynne's illustrations appear to be simple, they are, in fact, very specific and complicated. Critics often say that real artists tend to put reflections of themselves, their image, likeness, convictions and passions into their work. This is also true about Fred Gwynne.

Fred had a "love-hate" relationship with Herman due the strength and typecasting of the character which would slip into almost every area of his life far beyond the show. In later life Fred was quoted as saying, "And I might as well tell you the truth, I love old Herman Munster. Much as I try not to, I can't stop liking that fellow."

Even though we will always remember Fred as the giant bobble-headed Herman Munster and the southern judge with the one famous line, "Did you say two youts?!" that made the movie 'My Cousin Vinnie' such a hit, we can always be thankful that he left behind a series of books for our kids to love and enjoy for generations to come. The next time you read these books, try to imagine that incredible booming voice of his reading the words to you. While you're reading those words, always remember the giant talent that was behind them. Fred Gwynne was a true renaissance man.

A page from The King Who Rained, with a caricature of Fred Gwynne.
A page from Pondlarker and an article on the pun master.

MUNSTERS IN MUSIC
BY BUTCH PATRICK

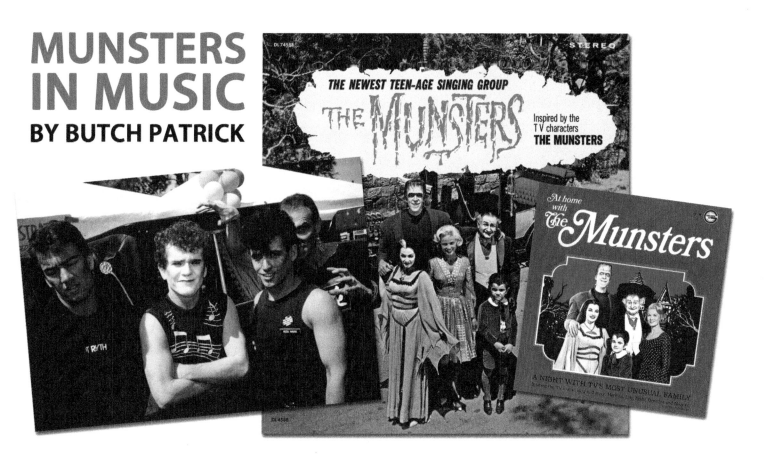

When Jack Marshall created the Munsters theme, no one could have imagined the longevity of that composition. Over 100 recordings at least. The London Philharmonic Orchestra, the Boston Pops, Brian Setzer Orchestra. Individual acts like Rob Zombie, Scum of the Earth, and even my cover tune *Whatever Happened To Eddie*. Yup, I'm proud to say WHTE was the first unsigned act ever to get a video on the upstart television network called MTV!!! It's funny that even though we never performed, people will sometimes say, "you were awesome at so-and-so festival", to which I say thank you and know it's great to be remembered. Even if it's imagined. I can relate, as I'm sure a few of my memories of the 60s might be a bit askew too. One thing IS for sure, whenever I'm around a band and they know I'm in the house, the Munsters theme is played. It seems EVERY guitar player in the world has picked up on that little riff! Music was such a big part of life in general that it wasn't a stretch to include it into the Munsters. We had the Standells guest on "Far Out Munster". Larry Tamblyn was kind enough to send in his very funny memory. I believe the Beatles once visited the set but I wasn't there that day :(. I've been told, although I can't substantiate, that Paul even watched The Munsters to relax. Fact or fantasy, either way 1964 was a great year for creativity on both sides of the pond for sure.

Fred Gwynne was known to play music on the set.
Here he is with the Standells.

I can remember that when the Standells were signed to perform on the Munsters, I was absolutely thunderstruck. This was my favorite TV show. I watched it faithfully every week. Amazingly, the episode "Far Out Munsters" was filmed in late 1964, about two years before we ever had our first hit record "Dirty Water", and long before we became teen idols. On the set, I discovered that the cast - Fred Gwynne, Yvonne De Carlo, Al Lewis, and of course Butch Patrick, were absolutely wonderful to work with. Right away, we hit it off with Butch, who today is a friend. At the time, I don't think Butch knew that his dialogue would prove to be prophetic. "But Pop, they're The Standells. Every kid in school is crazy about 'em. And they're coming to town for a concert. Boy, I'd give anything to meet 'em face-to-face." We had one particular scene that I remember to this day. It was during the beginning, when the Standells were meeting with their manager. There was a close-up of me talking while eating a banana. Well, I just couldn't get it right. I think it took about twenty takes to get it right, and in the process I must have consumed half a dozen bananas. Boy, was I sick afterwards.

-Larry Tamblyn

MUMY MUNSTER MEMORIES

It's funny how certain shows really resonate with people, while others are simply forgotten asterisks in a catalogue of work. "Come Back Little Googie", the episode of The Munsters that I guest starred in, has proven to be a well-remembered fan favorite. I remember filming it at Universal in early 1965, right after I had completed the pilot of Lost in Space. Working at Universal was always nice. I especially liked their commissary, and they had a little gift shop on the main street near the front gate that was run by a lady named Lorraine. I had fun hanging out for a few minutes every day with her.

Leave it to Beaver was always one of my favorite television series, and it remains at the top of my list to this day. "Come Back Little Googie" was written by Joe Connely and Bob Mosher, who of course created, wrote, and produced Leave it to Beaver, and they also produced The Munsters. The character I played, Googie, was a real trickster. Not a nice kid. I considered him to be like "Eddie Haskell" times ten.

Besides being impressed with the wonderful sets, I remember thinking the makeup process the cast went through on a daily basis was very intense, especially Fred Gwynn's. The episode included a chimpanzee, which was fun. It was a nice couple of days working alongside Butch Patrick.

Bill Mumy

One of Gene Trindl's unused photos for the TV Guide cover.

MY LIFE WITH THE MUNSTERS
BY GEORGE BARRIS

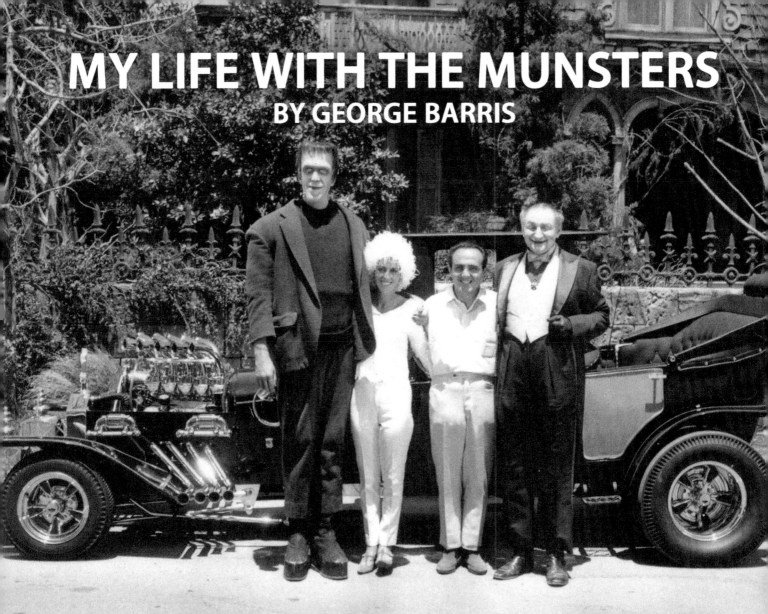

The producers of Universal Pictures contacted Shirley and I to make a Munster Koach for the new TV show "The Munsters". I went over and looked at the hearse they had designed and decided it was not unique enough for the Munster Family. I then looked at using a Model T for the Koach. I ended up using two Model T's so I would be able to get the 6 doors I needed for the Koach, so that the entire Munster Family could ride together.
I took photos which I cut and pasted and took them to the producer who said "there is one thing you have overlooked. . .where does the baby Eddie sit?"

Therefore I came up with the small bench that is attached to the back of the Koach. I added the tufted velvet seat for his comfort. Eddie was elevated so that he could see over everyone's head. He was a happy camper.
In later years, Butch Patrick and I toured the Munster Koach with the "World of Wheels". It was a big hit. Butch "Eddie" would sit in his tufted red seat for all to see. He will always be the one and only "Eddie Munster".
Butch would come to the Barris Kustom Shop every once in a while to check up on what new cool rides were being built.

George Barris

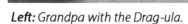

Left: *Grandpa with the Drag-ula.*
Top: *Butch with George Barris in a recent picture.*
Above: *The Munster Koach.*

In 1964, The Munsters were airing on TV. My brother and I were glued to the set as we watched Herman, Eddie, and the rest of the ghoulish cast trying to function in an everyday society. They were monsters that made us laugh, all our favorites including Frankenstein, Dracula, Wolfman and the Bride of Frankenstein. The costumes, make-up, scenery and most of all, The Munster Koach and Dragula added to the intrigue. The '60s was a time when drag racing came of age, and The Munsters Koach and Dragula were synonomous with drag racing. George Barris had to have had that in mind when he built them. We would buy them as 1/24 scale models from the local drug store and couldn't wait to get home to build them.

My interest in cars grew, and by the time I was sixteen I was well on my way to building Hot Rods, and eventually wound up with muscle cars. A 340 Plymouth Barracuda, four-speed hemi orange was my first car. I bought it in 1974, and still own it today, along with three more, all 1970 Plymouth Barracudas; a 383 plumb crazy (in violet) slap stick, a hemi with a Doug Nash 5 speed sublime (in limelight) and a 572 hemi orange nostalgic drag car that I purchased from a museum in Indiana. I brought all four cars to a car show in Fitchburg, Massachusetts, where I met George Barris. George came over to us and was interested in all the cars that my friends and I showed up with. We all instantly became friends and George gave us an open invitation to see the movie star collection of cars in California. I said to myself that I would take him up on it one day.

In January of 2002, I decided to go to an auction in Arizona. On the last day of the auction, I called George and asked if it would be ok if me and a friend could visit him. He said he would love to have us.

We arrived at a hotel just down the street from George's shop, and as I walked up to the hotel foyer I saw Lou Ferrigno (The Incredible Hulk) standing in the doorway. I dropped my bags in amazement and proceeded to walk in. Next, I ran into Clint Howard and next to him was Butch Patrick. I was dumbfounded. They were all doing an autograph signing and I couldn't get my pen out fast enough! I peaked Butch's attention when I told him I was there to see George Barris and check out the TV show cars, including the Munster Koach.

I told Butch that George's daughter Josi was coming to pick us up, and he asked to please bring her in as he grew up with her on the set of Universal Studios while The Munsters was filming. Josi invited us to dinner, including Butch, and we all had a great time. The next day, George gave us a tour of all the cars including the Munsters Koach, Dragula, Batmobile, Monkeemobile and countless others. It was a great experience to meet Butch and see the iconic car collection George had.

I gave Butch my phone number and told him if he was ever in Connecticut and needed a place to stay to look me up. Some years later I got a call from Butch and he told me he was in New York and I insisted he visit with me. Now every time he comes to the East coast he stays so much that he has his own room.

- Greg Franzino

71

I am affiliated with George Barris and Barris Kustom Ind., I've been in and around Barris Kustoms since the early '60s, and my story with Butch Patrick goes way back. I thought that the custom hot rod George built for the series was the most outrageous car I had ever seen. The coolest car ever built. Functional, and portrayed as an every day driver as well as a family car. Butch and I are close in age, so I related to him. Over the years working at Barris Kustoms, I had gotten to meet Butch, and I always thought he was pretty cool. We went through a lot of the same things in life both growing up in the entertainment industry. I never looked at Butch as a superstar and was never in awe about his role as Eddie Munster. He was a regular guy. We started traveling to different car shows and have made appearances around the country over the past 20 years. One thing I was impressed with, is that in the show Butch got to drive all sorts of cool things. One episode they built a custom go-kart, and there was a real cool gold chain link frame bicycle that is still around to

this day. Back to Butch, he has always been a sincere and honest guy. After all these years, we have become pretty close and I still try to do shows with him. It's always a good time when you are away from home and are with people that you know.

Back in 1966, the TV studios came once again to Barris Kustoms to build a crime-fighting car for a new TV series called 'Batman'. George Barris came through once again, and this time he built a car which turned out to become the most famous car in the world. I was also lucky enough to have been a part of that too, but I was a true hot rod guy and I always favored the famous "Munster Koach".

To this day, there are two Munster Koaches. The original one from the series, and another one built right after George Barris sold it. The second Koach is owned by Barris, and it has recently undergone a complete restoration, including a Rousch racing motor and 4 wheel disc brakes. The best part is that it is street legal so we are able to drive it on the street. This is the car that Butch does appearances with. It is a nice treat to see when children come up to the Koach and want to take a picture with it. Then when their parents see the car and Butch, it's a whole different ball game. The parents get more excited when Butch is around. It sort of brings them back to their childhood and they can reminisce.

I am glad that I am a friend of Butch Patrick, and feel very fortunate to have been a part of the history of this iconic TV show, The Munsters

- Tony Wood

Lion Drag Strip in Wilmington, CA. This strip was a popular Raceway in the 60's and the 70's until it shut down in 1972. The episode "Hot Rod Herman" was filmed there.

Top: "Country Club Munster."
Right: "All-Star Munster" with Pat Buttrum.

74

WHY THE MUNSTERS STILL HAUNT ME

BY KEVIN BURNS

In the August 21st issue of LIFE magazine, 1964 was touted as "TV's Year of the Monster."

I was nine years old at the time, and had already become hooked on Universal monsters – thanks to Aurora model kits, Famous Monsters of Filmland magazine and reruns of old horror films on Saturday nights.

As I thumbed through the gigantic black and white pages of the article, I saw lots of pictures of something called, "The Addams Family" (which left me cold, as they really didn't look much like monsters), a page of really cool monster toys (which quickly became my "must possess items for Christmas), and a HUGE full-page photo of Fred Gwynne made up to look like a smiling Frankenstein's monster!

I was hooked.

I knew from reading Famous Monsters that Universal had produced the original, classic horror movies with Boris Karloff, Bela Lugosi and Lon Chaney Jr. And when I found out that Universal would also be producing "The Munsters" I was eager to see an "official" TV series featuring my favorite classic creatures.

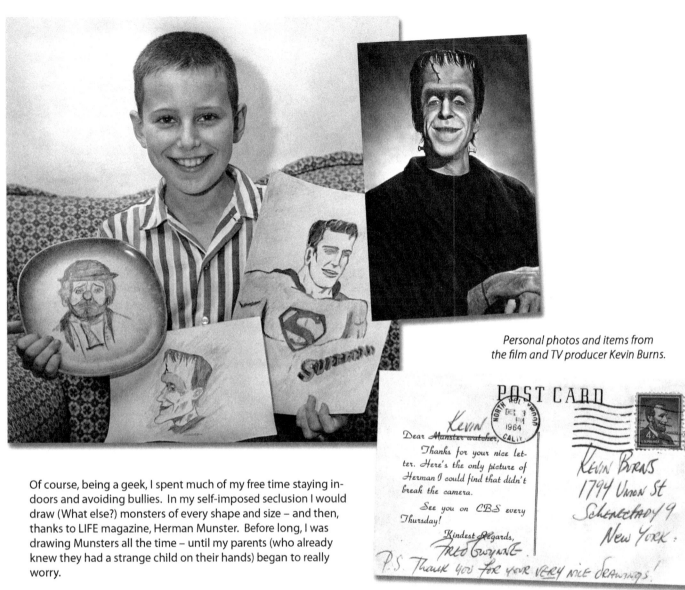

*Personal photos and items from
the film and TV producer Kevin Burns.*

Dear Munster watcher, Kevin

Thanks for your nice let-
ter. Here's the only picture of
Herman I could find that didn't
break the camera.

See you on CBS every
Thursday!

Kindest Regards,
Fred Gwynne

P.S. Thank you for your VERY nice drawings!

POST CARD

Kevin Burns
1794 Union St
Schenectady 9
New York.

Of course, being a geek, I spent much of my free time staying in-
doors and avoiding bullies. In my self-imposed seclusion I would
draw (What else?) monsters of every shape and size – and then,
thanks to LIFE magazine, Herman Munster. Before long, I was
drawing Munsters all the time – until my parents (who already
knew they had a strange child on their hands) began to really
worry.

On September 24, 1964, "The Munsters" premiered on Thursday
night at 7:30 PM on CBS. The episode was "Munster Masquer-
ade" and it was then that I knew that all of the weeks and weeks
of waiting had been worth it.

I kept drawing Munsters… on napkins… on placemats… even
on tablecloths.

One day, my worried mother read an article that said that Fred
Gwynne went to Harvard, had been the editor of the Harvard
Lampoon and had even written and illustrated children's books.
"Why don't you send some of your drawings to Fred Gwynne?"
she said. "Maybe he could give you some advice."

Drawing of the Munsters by Kevin Burns from 1968.

Now, the only other time I had ever written to a Hollywood celebrity was when I joined the Huckleberry Hound Fan Club five years earlier – and I really couldn't imagine why Fred Gwynne would care about some nine-year-old kid living in Schenectady, New York. Oh, well. What the heck. I carefully chose a few of my best drawings and sent them, along with a crudely written fan letter, to: "Fred Gwynne, care of Universal City Studios, Hollywood, California."

It was a simpler time in those days. No Zip Codes!

That Christmas, I got a lot of Munsters stuff. There were little Remco dolls of Herman, Lily and Grandpa… trading cards… puzzles… comic books… and even an Aurora Munsters model kit. But a few days later… as I was neatly stacking my holiday haul beneath the family tree, a postcard arrived in our mail slot. It was of Herman Munster. And on the back there was a printed message that read, "Dear Munster Watcher, **see you on** CBS every Thursday, Kindest Regards, Fred Gwynne" But "Munster Watcher" was crossed out and it said "Dear Kevin." There was even a P.S., that said, "Thank you for your *very* nice drawings."

Oh my gosh! It's from Fred Gwynne! Herman Munster wrote to me!" Then, my little nine-year-old brain started doing the forensics. "Is this really his signature? Did a secretary write it? Did this really come from him? If it came from him, he crossed out "Munster Watcher"! He put MY name in it!"

I practically slept with that postcard.

In the months following that fateful December day, I drew more Munsters pictures and got more notes of encouragement from

Fred Gwynne. I collected Munsters toys and comic books and scrounged photos and TV spots from the local TV station. When I was in high school in 1971, I even dressed up and put on my Don Post over-the-head latex Munster mask to perform as Herman in a charity-sponsored Haunted House. It was that same year that I bravely tracked down Fred Gwynne's phone number (it was listed, by the way) and called to thank him for a recent drawing he had sent me. "I'm going to be 'you' in a local haunted house," I sheepishly offered. "Well… I'll be damned," my hero responded. "Scare the hell out of 'em."

Kevin Burns as Grandpa with Hugh Hefner, George Barris and a group of playmates.

After going to college and film school I made my way out to Hollywood and worked for several years as an executive and in-house television producer at Twentieth Century Fox. By then I had personally met and befriended Fred, Al Lewis, Yvonne De Carlo, Butch Patrick, Pat Priest and Beverley Owen. I had also amassed a personal collection of "Munstermabilia" that could fill a large storage facility. (In fact, it does fill a large storage facility!)

In 1999, I received a phone call from one of the executives at A&E who asked if I would be interested in producing a "Biography" episode on Fred Gwynne. "Are you kidding?" I gasped. "Do you know who you're asking?"

Within the next few years I did profiles on Fred, Al, Yvonne and even one on "The Munsters" series itself.

(See, mom? All those years of drawing and collecting finally paid off!)

For me, "The Munsters" is not just a classic 1960s television show. It is not just a really cool retro-take on Frankenstein, Dracula and the Universal monsters. For me it represents a very real and very personal journey – stretching back to a time when I was a nine-year-old geek who loved things that were mysterious, visual and magical. It was a time of innocence -- and 12-cent comic books and soft drinks that cost a dime.

"The Munsters" – and the personal relationships I got to have with it – helped me through both good times and bad. It inspired me, motivated me and helped me remember that there are things in life that are not meant to do more than make us laugh.

By the way… in case you were wondering… I'm still a geek. And, hopefully, if you are reading this, you are too.

Kevin Burns at the Munster house on the Universal Studios back lot.

Top: Al Lewis with Kevin Burns
at a collectors show.
Far Right: A drawing of Herman
by Fred Gwynne.
Right: Guider Entertainment
and Restaurant Guide with
Kevin Burns in a Don Post mask.

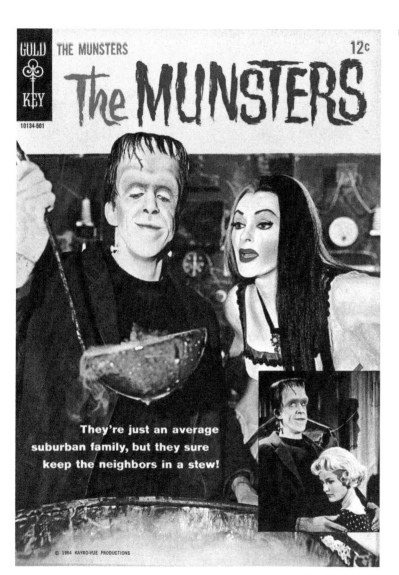

The Munsters #1

THE MUNSTERS IN COMICS

BY ROBERT J. SODARO

The Munsters acquired their very own comic book adaptation published by Gold Key, where16 issues were published ('65–'68). Additionally, a five-issue revival was published in '97 (four regular issues and a special convention issue) published by TV Comics. While the TV show had "typical" sitcom episodic adventures, the comic book was structured more like a typical Archie comic, with short vignettes depicting random comedic events in their lives — save for the final issue of the original run, which featured a full-length story broken up into three chapters. All of the stories tended to feature "monstrous" puns sprinkled throughout all of the stories. Interestingly enough, when the comic book initially appeared, the infamous Comics Code Authority was still in effect, and expressly forbade the appearance of vampires in comics. However, this proved to not be a problem at Gold Key, as the company wasn't a member of the Comics Magazine Association of America and thus didn't have to conform to the Code, allowing both Lily and Grandpa to appear in the comics without problems.

The comic's initial 16-issue run was published by Western's K.K. Publishing arm, under its Gold Key logo. The book's yeoman's chores (art, writing, lettering) was done by Fred Fredericks, with occasional help (towards the latter half of the series' run) by folks like Al Kilgore, Ben Oda, Joe Certa, Dan Adkins, Richard Bassford, Wally Wood, Mike Sekowsky, Paul Newman (no, not the actor), and Mel Crawford. As story credits were essentially non-existent at that time, none of the creators' names ever appeared in the

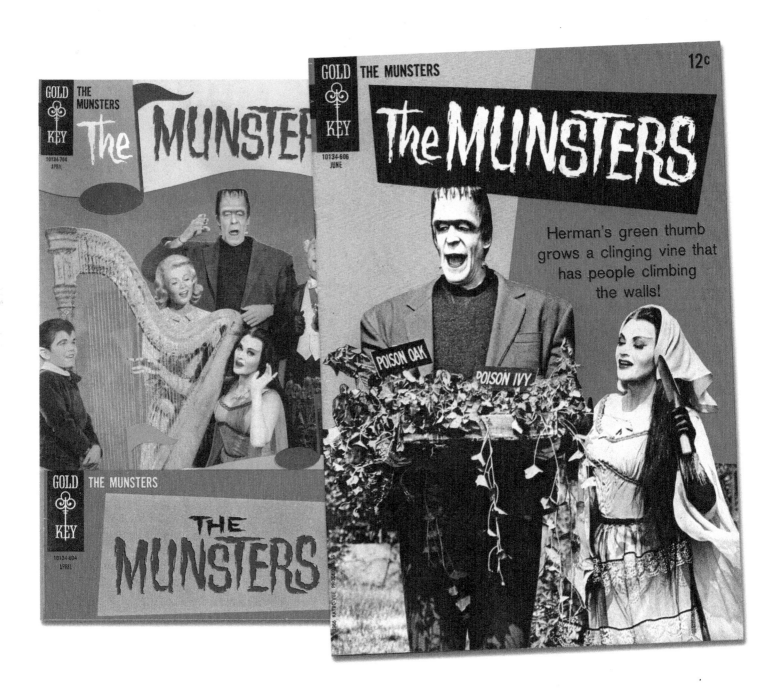

Munsters page from Gold Key Comics.

POSTMASTER: Please send notice on Form 3579 to K.K. Publications, Inc., North Road, Poughkeepsie, New York 12602. THE MUNSTERS, No. 16, February, 1968. Published quarterly by K.K. Publications, Inc., North Road, Poughkeepsie, New York 12602. Second-class postage paid at Poughkeepsie, New York. Subscription price in the U.S.A. 45c per year; foreign subscriptions 75c per year; Canadian subscriptions 60c per year. All rights reserved throughout the world. Authorized edition. Produced in U.S.A. by Western Publishing Company, Inc. Copyright © 1967, by Kayro-Vue Productions.

CHANGE OF ADDRESS should reach us four weeks in advance of the next issue date. Give both your old and new address enclosing if possible your old address label.

THE MUNSTERS #4 BY TV COMICS.

comics themselves (in fact, the issues themselves didn't even carry issue numbers, save for the indicias, and issue #1 had no issue number or month attached to it at all). Each issue in that initial run contained not only three 8-page Munster stories, but a four-page Liddle Wolfgang story. All 16 issues of the initial run were printed in color.

The Liddle Wolfgang short was about a young lad who would make his father crazy as the lad was fascinated by monsters (vampires werewolves, and goblins — oh my) and would spend his time either attempting to become a creature of the night, or spend his time attempting to locate one, much to his harried father's consternation.

THE MUNSTERS #1 by TV COMICS and THE MUNSTERS #2, art by
Doug Crane and Richard Maurizio.

All of the issues featured photo covers from the TV shows. Beginning with issue #8 the issues began adding in a one-page text "horror" story (usually with a twist ending) which allowed for some slightly longer Munster tales. In issue #12 other features were added, including a joke page, a couple of single pages stocked with two and three panel gags, and a monster museum page. The 1997 TV Comics revival differed from the Gold Key run in that each issue contained a full-length story and (like the TV show itself) was printed in glorious Black & White. The initial issue was a special one-shot that was produced for the 1997 San Diego Comic Con International, and was 24 pages in length. Like the original run, each story was full of monster puns, sight gags, and a fair share of in-jokes. The entire five issues were later collected into a trade paperback. These issues featured interviews and text articles as well as photo covers. The TV Comics were produced by Kelley Jarvis, Richard Maurizio, Marc Patten, George Broderick, Charles Barnett, III and JT Studios (Special Edition) and C.J. Henderson, Kevin Cleary (writers) Broderick, Doug Crane, Art Nichols, Brad Gorby (Pencilers), Barnett, Maruizio, Jim Amash, Mark Heike (Inkers), Bob Pinaha, Rebecca Black (Letters) for the regular series.

In re-reading the Gold Key issues we discovered a couple of very interesting incongruous continuity errors. In the story *Just Plane Crazy* which appeared in issue #6, a sky diver lands in the Munster's back yard and states that he is just 45 minutes out of

A promotional piece for TV COMICS illustrated by Kelley Jarvis and Richard Maurizio.

Brooklyn, and is surprised to find what he initially thought were cannibals (he fell into an open cauldron in which Lily was making soup). However, according to the Munster's Wikipedia entry, Mockingbird Heights is a fictional suburb located somewhere in California. This error is repeated in *A Fright for Sore Eyes* (in issue #8). While Herman is wearing a gorilla suit (and grown large due to a spell by Grandpa), he makes his way into Manhattan and winds up climbing the Empire State building, as did King Kong.

This is all well and good, and could be chalked up to the fact that the TV show was produced in California and the comic in New York, so each creative team simply drew upon their own locale. However in issue #16, during the race to Transylvania, a map clearly shows Herman and Grandpa starting off somewhere in Oklahoma or Kansas. Even stranger, after crossing into Russia they make their way into Turkey, wind up driving up through Italy, and passing through Switzerland before arriving in Transylvania. Given that Transylvania is part of Romania (which is separated from Turkey by Bulgaria), how both men wound up in Italy (at the bottom, which is across the Mediterranean Sea, just the other side of Greece) is something of a mystery.

One can only assume that the writers either didn't know their geography (or the show's fictional location of Mockingbird Heights), or figured that as it was a kid's comic book things like that didn't actually matter, or they simply didn't care. In the TV Comics revival, more care was paid to these types of issues (witness the family flying into NY in issue #2).

Above: Gold Key issue 16 "Race to Transylvania."

The following pages are from an unpublished story written by C.J. Henderson, with pencils by Ben Fogletto. Note: the correction marks by the art director.

MUNSTERS COLLECTIBLES

BY ROBERT J. SODARO

When talking about the iconic '60s TV show The Munsters, the discussion must naturally cover all of the amazing (and unusual) collectibles that were generated off the show, especially considering that it only lasted two years on the air (and then ran for-freaking-ever in syndication). Tony Greco is a seriously hardcore Munsters fan, and has amassed both a great deal of knowledge about the collectibles and acquired many of them over the years as well. According to Greco, the Top ten Munster's Collectibles are as follows:

1. Bowling game (there is a question among collectors if it actually exists)
2. Numbered Pencil & Paint set
3. Paint-A-Plaque
4. Hypo-Squirt gun
5. Kite
6. Jewelry
7. Buttons from Warren Publishing of Herman, Lily, and Eddie
8. Ben Cooper Grandpa Munster costume ("When you were a kid who the hell wanted to be dressed as an old man?" says Greco)
9. Wrist flashlight
10. "The Munster" Car Coat

Munsters toys were heavily marketed from 1964–1966. Some of the top manufactures of Munsters toys and books were Remco, Hasbro, Ideal, and of course Western Publishing which also published The Munsters' comic book.

Remco came out with a series of big head dolls featuring The Munsters; it also had similar series based on The Beatles, The Dave Clark Five, The Addams Family, and more. These dolls were about 5" tall with the head itself about two inches. The heads were made of rubber and had hair. Mattel offered up a talking Herman doll and hand puppet. The doll and puppet came in different variations. Of course there's also a Munsters Marilyn Munster doll that came from Japan. She's 11 inches tall and wears an orange dress with white shoes. The packaging on the toy is a cardboard box with a label with Pat Priest's photo with the text Marilyn Munster pasted on it.

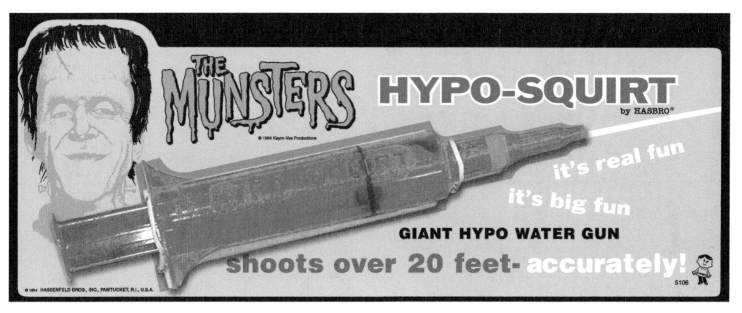

Ideal came out with the Mini-Monster dolls in 1965 and 1966; the dolls were based on Herman, Lily, Eddie, and Woof Woof, but with the names of the characters changed because the Munsters show had been canceled. There were also Munster Colorforms, which came with two different packaging designs; one was a larger size box and there was a smaller version as well. As stated, Western Publishing produced comics, but it also published coloring and storybooks. Aurora came out with the Munsters living room model kit, which was one of the hardest models to put together with its tiny pieces, especially including the wires to assemble Grandpa's electric chair.

During the '70s, there weren't very many Munsters-related items, save for a few T-shirts and smaller items. It was during this time that the show still remained in syndication.

One of the rarest Munsters collectibles is the Hypo-squirt gun.

The made-for-TV movie, The Munsters' Revenge came out in 1981 and sparked a new interest in the show, especially with the release of the VHS tape into the burgeoning video aftermarket. Still, the real resurgence for the Munsters didn't pick up until the Munsters Today TV revival was put into syndication from '88 to '99.

There was a promo from A&W Root Beer with a giant-size Herman blow-up, which has become quite a sought after collectible. Service Merchandise also used Herman's image, as did McDonald's, which did a campaign with Classic TV characters including Grandpa in the early 1990s. Presents, a company owned by Applause, came out with a series of dolls and PVC figures based on the Munsters. Then Hostess put the Munsters on their advertising boxes. Promotional items from the campaign have proven to be very collectible. With the release of Here Come the Munsters in 1995 (yet another Munsters TV movie) and the

boom in the collectibles market, The Munsters became a very sought-after property; spawning dart flip cards, Star Jars, and an brand new comic book from TV Comics.

The Danbury Mint released Herman and Lily, as well as a mail-order Grandpa. M&Ms had a campaign with Munsters in the early 2000s. Current Munster collectibles include the following:

• Tweeterhead Maquettes released a special edition 15" Herman Munster Marquette, with a black and white edition of 313 pieces, and a Lily limited to 113 pieces.

• Diamond Select produced a black and white figure set- a variant version came with the whole family, in a boxed set. Individual characters on a blister card came painted in color.

• Moibius came out with Herman, Grandpa, and Munsters' House models this year.

The one question amongst collectors is: Does the bowling game that was seen in catalogues in the sixties actually exist? According to Tony Greco, it does, while other collectors, including Kevin Burns, claim that it doesn't. Ultimately, it is the adulation of the fans that keep this show and its collectibles alive, and continue to bring it back into the public eye. Hopefully, renewed interest will generate new collectibles, comics, and perhaps even a new TV show.

Top Ten Munsters Collectibles

1. Bowling game (there is a question among collectors if it actually exists)
2. Numbered Pencil and Paint Set
3. Paint-A-Plaque
4. Hypo-Squirt gun
5. Kite
6. Jewelry
7. Buttons from Warren Publishing of Herman, Lily, and Eddie
8. Grandpa Munster Halloween Costume
9. Wrist flashlight
10. Car coat

3034-6 – MUNSTER BOWLING SET Those "monstrously" funny Munsters are all lined up to serve as pins for this fun-filled new bowling game. Made of sturdy, colorful plastic are spiffy Grampa, loving Lily and Herman, plus sweet little Eddy. Complete with 2 bowling balls.

Pack per doz.: 1   Wgt.: See price list.

This is the **Holy Grail** of Munsters toys. The *Munster Bowling Set* only appeared in a sales catalogue. Collectors dispute if IDEAL ever released it. To this day it has never been found.

Photos © Park Lane Drive Productions.

I have fond memories of growing up watching one of my all-time favorite shows "The Munsters." I consider myself lucky to have watched them the first time they aired on CBS television, on Thursday nights I believe. Then, I loved watching them as reruns for many years after, and sometimes my friends and I would watch the show after school. My family and I took the Universal Studios tour in the Summer of 1968. We passed by the Munsters' house riding the tour tram. When the tour was over, one of my earliest thrills was to meet Grandpa Al Lewis. I still remember to this day telling him that my friends and I watched him on TV and he said that he was able to watch US through the magic of television! He said, "I can see you and your friends sitting on the living room floor", and he then started to laugh like Grandpa! Many years later, I got to know him when he opened his restaurant in New York City. He would occasionally invite me to sit with him at his table and chat. I am also both proud and honored to have become good friends with Butch Patrick after producing the CD recording of the song "It's Only Halloween" and the music video DVD. Never in my wildest dreams did I ever imagine that I would get to know some of my favorite Munsters.

-Henry Golis and Ann-dee

Thanks, loved working on CD with you and Ann-dee.

I was born in October of 1964, just 20 days after the very first episode of The Munsters aired (original air date: Sept 24,1964). I grew up in the city of Detroit, MI. My favorite time of year was always October and Halloween. During Halloween, every house in our neighborhood had a porch light on to greet trick or treaters. Your mother made your costume, and you always came home with a huge bag full of candy! With my love for Halloween, I would gravitate towards shows like The Munsters. I would watch the show in reruns on our local Detroit TV station every day after school. When I was 9 years old, my parents agreed to allow me to have my first pet dog, and my father knew a family that bred Yorkshire Terriers. We went as a family and my parents allowed me to pick a male puppy. When the breeder asked me what I was going to name my new puppy, I already had a name chosen. I said "Herman", naming him after the head of the Munster household. Herman lived to be 16 1/2 years old and was the best friend a boy could have. I still enjoy Halloween to this day and have over 900 trick or treaters come to my door. I actually met Butch Patrick on my recent trip to Salem, Mass. during Halloween 2013. I do have to wonder- has my love for Halloween attracted me more to the Munsters…or did watching The Munsters build my fondness for Halloween?

-Jerry Kovach (Monroe, Michigan)

Henry Golis, Butch Patrick and Marky Munster.

101

My favorite memory is Herman throwing Eddie through the ceiling!
I thought that was real!! What a hoot!!
-Simon B.

That was fun!

Always getting the house together to watch the Munsters while we ate dinner.
-Natalie T.

TV dinners, TV sets and wholesome viewing in the sixties. Good Times!

How Herman always took time to be a good father to Eddie.
-Vince H.

Loved our Father/Son talk shows.

Herman scared me!
-Keryl H.

Sorry, but he was so lovable.

When the salesmen and people would go to 1313 Mockingbird Lane and get frightened and run away!!
-Marsha R.

Classic episodes.

The makeup was astounding!!
-Shelia M.

Westmores at their best!

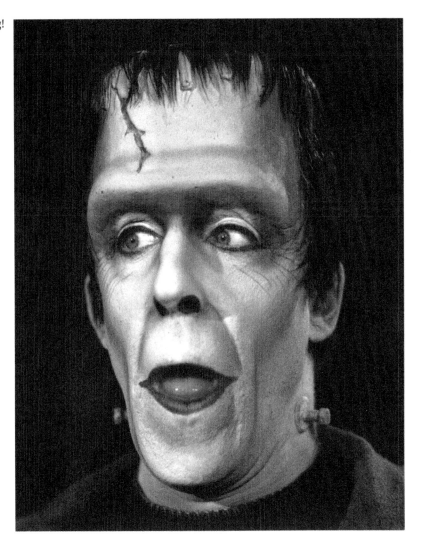

"I OWE IT ALL TO THE MUNSTERS"

AN INTERVIEW WITH TONY GRECO
BY RICHARD MAURIZIO

> *Tony Greco is one of the top authorities and collectors of Munsters memorabilia. We caught up with him at his home, or as he calls it, the Munsters Museum.*

Question: What got you into The Munsters?

TONY GRECO: Well, in the early sixties Universal sold their horror movies into syndication to TV stations, and there was a local TV show in Pittsburgh called Chiller Theatre with Chilly Billy Cardilli. At the age of 4 or 5, my fascination was with monsters. I loved them, but I was scared of them.

When The Munsters came on, it taught me that monsters weren't scary…they were wonderful! They looked different from every-body else, and that was my attraction to them. In the first season, there was an episode called Eddie's Nickname, where Eddie came home from school crying and Herman asked him what was wrong and he said they called him a terrible name. Herman asked,"What's that?",and Eddie replied, "Shorty", for no good reason other than he was the shortest kid in class. I could relate to that because I was the shortest in my class, even though they never called me Shorty. So Grandpa gave him a potion and he grew a beard, but at the end, he's sitting on Herman's lap and Herman tells him it doesn't matter what color you are…if you're fat or skinny, tall or short, handsome like your father or ugly, the only thing left that matters is the size of your heart and the strength of your character, and I live my life like that and it made life a whole lot easier.

Tony Greco and his Dragula.

Q: The show did show moral values, even though they were monsters…

TG: Yes, and that's it. Good family values-funny and nothing ever controver-sial. Since I was a little kid, I've loved the Munster Koach. There was a hobby shop in downtown Pittsburgh called Bill & Walt's. When I was nine or ten, I'd take a streetcar into town and would go and look in the window where they had a built Munster Koach model. Every time I would go in they would be out of them, so I would always offer to buy the display model and they wouldn't sell it! So when I was twelve, I'd still go there. Then one day I looked and it was gone. I freaked out and I walked around and looked in the side window and was relieved it was still there. About a year later it was gone for good and I went in and said, "Walt, where's the car?" He said they threw it out and I was so sick about it! So, that may have intensified my Munsters collecting.

Q: This was the AMT model?

TG: Yes, the 1/25th scale one. I loved that car, so I collected the toys from The Munsters. In '64, '65 and then all of the sudden it was off the air. When I was a child I didn't quite understand why they took [shows] off.

Q: Wasn't it because of color? Batman came on in color and most of the shows went to color.

TG: Yes. With Batman and everything else going to color, I don't think it would have ever worked as good in color and that is actually why they took the show off and they didn't want to pay the difference in cost for color.
In the 1980s, there was a resurgence with The Munsters' Revenge but It wasn't the same as the old show.

Q: Would you say it was off and the writing wasn't there?

TG: Yes, But then when they came out with Munsters Today in '88, we almost wished for The Munsters' Revenge.

Q: I watched a few episodes of Munsters Today, but I do like 1995's Here Come the Munsters.

TG: Well, yeah, that's pretty good. It's as close as you can get. There's this restaurant out in California-it's called Cafe Buna,

and every time I'm out in L.A., my friend Kevin and I have to go there and eat because that's where Fred and Al were in The Munsters' Revenge, where they were dressed up as waitresses, but we just go in there and reminisce about it. Those are my memories of The Munsters, all things good, it was monsters and it was fun all rolled into one.

Q: With your love of the show and your fascination with it, did you meet any members of the cast prior to the '80s?

TG: Over the years, I've met the whole cast. Back in the '70s and '80s, I'd run into Fred every now and then.

Q: How was he towards you? Because it's known he was reluctant to talk about The Munsters.

TG: Fred was cordial, and he never refused me. I knew where not to push his buttons. Fred was worried about being stereotyped, and he didn't like that, but what he had to understand was that he was Herman Munster. Herman Munster and Fred Gwynne were one. He was perfect to play that part, almost too good, and he outdid himself. Looking back on it I'm sure he understood that.

I hear parents tell me all the time that they watch The Munsters together with their kids. They laugh and have a good time. They don't ever have to worry about them getting any type of bad influence.

Q: I finally watched the show with my eight-year-old daughter and she loved it. So getting back to the cast?

TG: Kids love it, they really do. Fred's goofy and he's lovable, but getting back to the cast, around 1988 Al opened up Grampa's, a restaurant in New York, and of course that gave me a reason to go to New York. Me and Di, my wife, would stay on West 44th street. We would go down to the village and she would do the laundry and I would go down and sit with Al. It just so happened in '88 that he was doing Super Scary Saturdays on TBS. There was a special with Butch, Pat and Al, almost in character, watching old Munsters episodes. Al and I talked about that.

Q: And at this time you were still collecting Munsters?

TG: Yeah, then in 1989 a company called Presents came out with the Munsters dolls. We're down on Sanibel Island, on vacation one day, right off the coast of Florida, and we went into a little gift shop. Diane was looking at some shells and other stuff and I went up to the register and there is a little Lily PVC. I asked what else they had there, and she showed me the dolls. I bought everything they had. I didn't care about Florida, I didn't

Some of the photos from Tony Greco's collection.

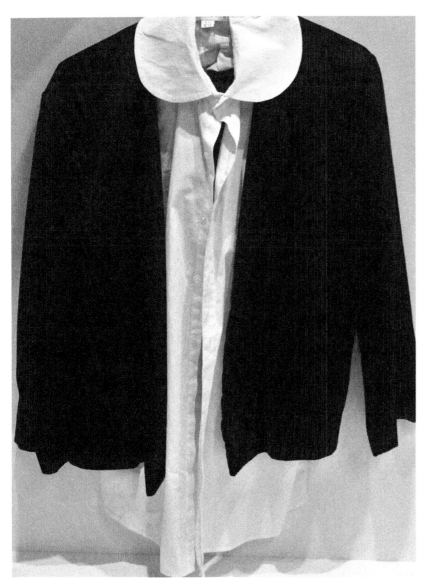

The Eddie Munster costume Butch Patrick wore for a Little Caesars Pizza commercial.

care about Sanibel, I had Munster toys (laughter). Twenty-five years later, it brings back a lot of fond memories, and right then and there it showed how much I loved The Munsters. Steven Cox also came out with a book about The Munsters. I didn't know anything about Kevin or anything, but in the book I saw that there was someone as goofy as me. I thought I was weird and I thought I was a freak. I'm in my thirties, going on forty, still playing with toys! I saw everything he had and I dug out my stuff from my mother's house, got it together and dusted it off. I wondered if I could track more of this stuff down, and I found out there was this newspaper called Toy Shop. In it, there were ads for cars and toys. That newspaper was the greatest thing in the world. I read it from front to back. Sometimes when you called for an item it would be gone, but I would find Munsters stuff in there and I would go to flea markets and I would buy different things here and there. Now, with the advent of the internet, that opened a whole new world, but it was also a double-edged sword. You could find anything you wanted on Ebay, but just when you thought you had the only one, there were a thousand others out there. So when you thought what you had was priceless, it wasn't.

Q: Wasn't there a story about one Munsters item that sold for a tremendous amount of money and a month later twenty or thirty showed up on the internet?

TG: There was a color-by-number set that showed up, and then Western Publishing ended up having a whole

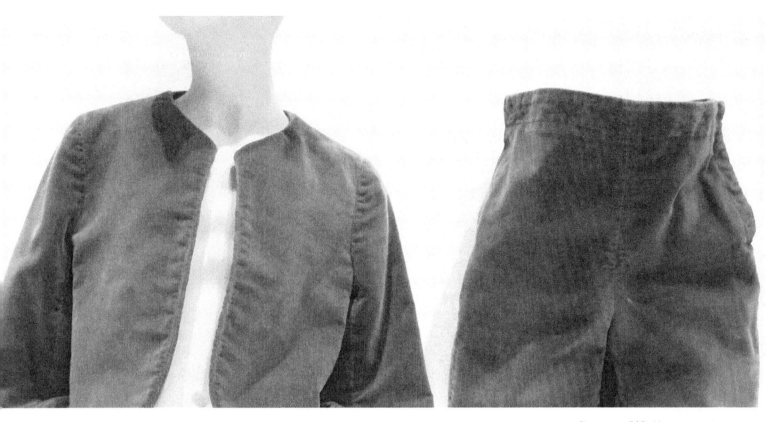

First season Eddie Munster costume.

case of them. I bought a few, Kevin bought a few. At the time, really good Munster stuff was going for 3, 4, 500 bucks. People would email me and I told them I didn't even know this existed. I wanted one, but if two people bid against each other this would drive the item price up, but that's when I became friends with Kevin. In the late 90's, Kevin would bid against me on a bunch Munsters stuff. So, I got in touch with him and said, "Look, we shouldn't have to bid against each other, 'cause I think it would raise the price on it." It just so happens, at the time I got to be friends with Butch (Patrick) at the Boston Munsters' Family Reunion, in 1996, and I told him a couple of stories. He thought I was full of crap, but then he found out what I told him was true

and so then he said to me, "Hey, I have this friend, Kevin Burns (that's the guy I'd been on the internet with)." I talked to Kevin on the phone, and we made an agreement. We decided that we weren't gonna fight against each other. Let's just say that my home is Kevin's East Coast home and his guest house in Beverly Hills is my West Coast home. We consider our collections the East Coast collection and the West Coast collection. He comes here and I'd go there and we would look at stuff and watch 16-milli-meter prints. Who else is going to do that? If you don't love them, you're not going to do that. We'd talk ten, twenty, thirty times a day about Munsters. So we basically figure them as one big collection, and now we would like to put it all in a big museum. Kevin actually has the blueprint to the Munsters' house and the inside floor plan. The inside and the outside don't match, but we want to build Munster house and put all the stuff in it. Well, I'm 56 now and have been retired for quite a few years, and every day I look at the Munsters stuff. I go downstairs and that's what makes me happy, because I remember it was all things good. I don't have to go down and pick anything up I just look, and that's why I open my home. Not to complete strangers, but people contact me and ask if they can come and see the Munster stuff. I've had people from England come over and have seen the collection and they are amazed. I love showing it off and I'm proud of it. I'm proud of what I've accomplished with it, and I basically want to make it like a memorial for The Munsters. My love for it goes beyond that. There's my family, The Munsters, then everything else I have. That's how high it is in my life, because it makes me happy. I try to explain to people when they ask me what I do for a living. I play with toys! That's what I do. I tell people all the time, if you do what you love, you'll never work a day in your life.

Q: So what would you say is your fondest memory?

TG: Basically, what The Munsters means to me are all things good. Over the years, I've met a lot of people. Butch has stayed here on and off over ten to fifteen years. I love Butch. He played the part perfectly. Nobody could have played Eddie Munster like he did. Those are my fondest memories. I couldn't say just one memory in particular, because I could watch it 10, 20, 30 times a week. It doesn't matter. I never get tired of it. People ask me why I watch it so much and I say I'm waiting for the ending to change, that's all. Getting back to the collectibles…

Q: You said the car is what you liked as a kid, but what was the first collectible?

TG: I don't remember. Back in '64, Kevin remembers the Remco dolls. I can't remember the first activity set. I had Colorforms and I had puzzles.

Orignal art of Lily by Andy Price, part of Tony Greco's collection.

108

Q: But that's when you were a child. When did you decided, "Hey I'm going to start collecting this stuff."?

TG: Well, some people don't understand, and I try to explain it. When you're a kid, you're not collecting. You're just playing with your toys. When it goes off the air and you go looking for something purposely, that's collecting. You accumulate stuff, but when you go looking for something that you can't get anymore, something that has been off the air 10 or 20 years, like Married With Children (I liked that show), you start collecting. So I explain to people that my first Munsters piece was in 1964, but I didn't start collecting until 1967, because the Munsters were off the air and then I went out looking. I didn't understand it as collecting at the time, but when I got something, I would buy it and get two- one to save, 'cause I always liked looking at the stuff, and one to play with or read, like the comic books. I tell people all the time, I've never thought of a Munsters item as an investment. I bought it because I love it. Yes, condition is everything, but there are a lot of people who love The Munsters and they don't care what kind of shape it's in. Don't go in debt collecting what you want. Buy what you can afford and enjoy it, and that way if you can't sell it and make money, look at it and like it. That's my biggest crack about collecting. I don't sell anything and it just accumulates. That's why I had to build a garage out back (laughter).

Q: Let's talk about your prized possession, The Dragula?

TG: When I found the Dragula, my wife said, "You know, that's the most useless thing you've ever bought" and I said I bought it to drive, because my Dragula was a real coffin and was eighty or ninety percent as accurate as the original, but the difference is you can drive mine. It's dependable. Now she says I can drive it and she can bury me in it. Now someone will probably try to come and dig it up (laughter)! So that was the climax to my collecting, when I got the Dragula. I love that car! I have it on display at a restaurant for people to see and enjoy seeing it.

Ray Jolle, owner of the Pittsburgh Quaker Steak and Lube.

Q: So would you consider yourself the top expert on The Munsters?

TG: There is nobody in the world besides Kevin and I that know more about The Munsters. What he doesn't know I know and what I don't know, he does. This is the funniest thing- Kevin owns Grandpa's electric chair and Lily's bat necklace and this and that, and when I told him we got a Dragula, he said, "I quit, I quit." But I'm happy for him and he's happy for me, and it has affected our lives in more ways than you could ever imagine. Because to me, I can say the Munsters are real, but only in a certain form. It's how people really are, but that just goes to show you that the only thing in life that matters is the size of your heart and the strength of your character and it doesn't matter what you look like. So, that's my story and I'm sticking to it. Life's been good to me and I owe it all to The Munsters.

My earliest memories of the Munsters start when I was sitting home one day bored out of my mind and my netflix actually gave me the Munsters as a suggestion. So I began to watch an episode, and before I had known it I blew through all 70 and I kept re-watching them over and over. I'd tell you who my favorite characters are, but it's almost impossible to choose. I enjoy watching Grandpa and Herman go at it and watching Lily try to keep order in the house. I've always been able to relate myself to Eddie, though. Through my school years I always was the outsider and wished there was a true Munster family out there so that I wasn't alone. The Munsters, to me, were the perfect family, how they never let anything bother them or break them up and how nothing seemed to be too big of a problem that it couldn't be solved. Herman would always manage to get into trouble, but just the same he would find a way out. Like in my favorite episode "Hot Rod Herman", when he loses the family car and with Grandpa's help gets it back no problem. That always made me feel like no matter what kind of trouble I get into, there's always a solution. I now have a pretty decent Munsters collection which I am very proud of. I've even had Lily tattooed on my arm. Me and my family watch them every night at dinner, and there's something to be said about a show that after 50 years can still be just as funny and still manage to get a family together. I still wish that there would have been more episodes, but at the same time the original '64-'66 Munsters hold a special place in my heart and always will! -

-Patrick McEwen (Rochester, New York)

A LITTLE HOUSE IN TEXAS

Charles and Sandra McKee built **The Munster Mansion** in *Waxahachie, Texas, and they open the house for tours and a special charity event each October.*

Question: Tell me where you got the idea to build a Munsters House?

SANDRA McKEE: Well, the idea really started just as a joke. We were restoring old houses. I was joking with my husband and I said it would be cool if we could build a Munster house. He said yeah, we could do that and I wanted to do it as fast as we could because I wanted to see how far we could take it.

Q: I did look online at your website a little bit, and noticed that you have a lot of antiques and items very authentic to the television show. As a collector, I go to out to flea markets and everything else. Where did you get some of those items?

SM: I found a lot of things on the internet. We do a lot of flea markets and tag sales because I do love antiques. For me, I've been searching for years- I just found furniture and different things over the years. We built this house twelve years ago, so it's been a twelve-year process. I also have a lot of friends that are Munsters fans that would call me and help me find things.

Q: In the television show, everything was so elaborate, but because it was in black and white you really couldn't see that much detail. Did you use photos or just the episodes? Were the DVDs out at the time?

SM: We used the VHS tapes. We had to make blueprints to the house from watching all the episodes. We didn't know where things were supposed to be and we had to figure out basically where things had to go for me to put everything in place.

The stairway at the McKee's house where everyone's Favorite pet will greet you.

111

Lily in the dining room with a plate full of Halloween cookies.

We had to make things a little bit bigger because they couldn't get everything in the exact way it was suppose to be, so things had to be built a little bit bigger. Lily and I are about the same size, so we would count the steps she would take to the living room or the kitchen, and we would use this as a way to space things out.

Q: Wow, that's a lot of detail you have to look into. Do you and your husband build houses? Or you built one house?

SM: No. He's a handyman and we had to do a lot of things ourselves, so when we started to do the house we had to have a builder start the construction part. So all we had when we started was the frame and structure

we did all the rest ourselves – the plumbing, the electrical, and everything else.

Q: Did you actually get to see the Munster House at Universal?

SM: Yes, I did, but it was the end result. We started the house in November of 2001, and finished it in 2002. Then in 2005, I saw the Munster house at Universal, but at the time they were using it for Desperate Housewives, so it looked different. It would've been nice to see something before.

Q: So you never saw anything except the VHS tapes for reference before you actually built the house?

SM: Unfortunately, no. We just started building the house and we started meeting people and didn't realize how many fans were out there. The fans were really helpful with things. It's just amazing and I can't even describe how wonderful it is to know how many people are out there that are Munsters fans.

Q: I was surprised myself.

SM: The fans are wonderful, and it's such a good show and a clean show. I think the younger generation needs to watch it. It's still funny and wonderful and we can still enjoy it today.

Q: I've been reviewing all the episodes for this book and it still holds up today. A lot of shows of that era don't hold up anymore.

SM: Any time we're doing an event, we sit down and watch the show over and over again, so we know what we need to do. That's just part of it. Last week was our anniversary, and we had no TV, so we took our laptops and we watched the show.

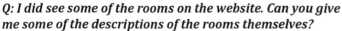
Some of the fine detail in the kitchen of the Munster Mansion.

Most of the rooms are exact, except we added an extra bedroom. We had to have one room for ourselves and didn't want to sleep on an old iron bed, so we have a comfortable King-size bed. There are some things I don't have because I can't find them as identical or as close to the show.

Q: You must have had the big can and other props custom-made?

SM: A friend of mine did, and he also comes down and has acted as Grandpa Munster. He made the gigantic size can opener and he made the clock for me. He's done a lot of things for me. He came to the first event in 2002 while Butch was here, and he comes back every single year for our event. It's really important, and a lot of people might not know this sort of thing, but for the fans that do, that's what's important to me.

Q: It's a great idea that you had and sounds really nice. Where in Texas are you located?

SM: Thirty minutes Southeast of Dallas.

Q: I did see some of the rooms on the website. Can you give me some of the descriptions of the rooms themselves?

SM: Sure, The house has a living room, fireplace, four bedrooms and two and a half baths. You enter into a big entryway and then we have a dining room with the table. Then you go by the stairs where Spot is, and in the living room are the organ and Grandpa's electric chair and the couch. I found an exact organ like the TV show. We also built the hidden entry where Eddie would go into the kitchen.

Q: It's also great that you are doing this all for a charity event too.

SM: We only do this two days a year, but people want us to do it more often (laughter), but we only do it two days a year because it's our home. We get everybody to come out and do the tour, then get autographs and we have a costume contest and

Butch with Sandra as Lily.

face painting...It's a big event for two nights.

We've had Grandpa out here and Pat and Butch come out here all the time.

The funny thing is, I would sit and think to myself when Butch stays in Eddie's room, "WOW, Eddie Munster is sleeping in Eddie's bedroom!"

Q: I can imagine what he's thinking while sleeping next to that big cage (laughter). You're on a lot of tourist websites. Do you have a lot of people in front of the house taking pictures all day?

SM: I usually keep the gate closed because of my dog, and people do maintain their distance since it is a tourist attraction and we don't want people to just go on in the house. I also have to keep the gate closed because of me freaking out when I look downstairs and there are people in my living room. People are all the way down there outside the gate taking pictures, and when I leave the gate open people come in on the grounds and take pictures and they do what they want to do. I have so many people ask me if there is any way they can get a tour. Because of an agreement with my husband, we won't do that, and if we did once, then we would have to start giving people tours all the time. It's just hard because I don't want anybody coming in my house unless it's exactly the way I want it to be. We live here, so I don't think we could open it up as a business, because restrictions wouldn't allow it.

Q: Well, I can understand that. Thanks you for your time. The Munster Mansion is South of Dallas, open two days a year in October, with proceeds going to charity.

A scene from the episode "Heap Big Herman."

MARKY MUNSTER:
THE ORIGINAL COLLECTOR
AN INTERVIEW WITH MARK DOYLE

Mark Doyle, also known as Marky Munster, has been collecting Munsters memorabilia for over thirty years. His collection includes a vast collection of photos, toys, and some of the rarer Munster items. Besides The Munsters, Mark is also one of the top Gilligan's Island collectors.

Question: Mark, How did you get the name Marky Munster?

Mark Doyle: Actually, I was in a garage band and a band member started calling me Marky Munster. At the time I was getting my first email and I chose Marky Munster@ so and so. I carried the name on and used it to contact fans, buy items, and built the website markymunster.com. Everyone now knows me by that name, and whenever I see Butch it's " Hey Marky Munster". So the name has taken on a whole life of its own.

Q: What got you into The Munsters?

MD: When I was five it was on TV and I fell in love with the show. I'm not a baby boomer but it was on 9 A.M. on channel 11 PIX New York. At times I actually missed the school bus to watch The Munsters. So I sacrificed my younger education to see the Munsters. (laughter)

Q: That's more important (laughter). Let's talk about your collection.What got you started?

MD: I've always been a collector. My mom always collected things, so I get it from my mom. When I was a kid I collected a

Mark Doyle with Al Lewis at Grampa's and years later with Pat Priest.

ton of toys, mainly the super-hero stuff. I had a lot of Batman and Planet of the Apes items. They were played with and weren't saved. When I was twelve or so KISS came onto the scene and I was hooked on them instantly. I was too old to play with the KISS figures and toys so I just collected them. I ended up selling the collection years later to start my Munsters collection. I really didn't know what was out there at the time and it wasn't until the first Steve Cox book came out that I saw a picture of someone (Kevin Burns) with his collection. I was surprised by how many Munsters items there were, and that got the blood flowing to start my collection.

Q: What was you first item?

MD: I was in New Jersey and I picked up a T-shirt, and that was my first piece. Back then the flea markets were good and you could find things cheap. The first sixties piece I got was the puzzle. When I got home I stared at that and looked at that for hours. (laughter)

Q: Was there a piece you chased after?

MD: I always wanted the Aurora model kit. When I got it I had it professionally built and then went on to find other items. I like to collect the more obscure stuff like the 45 records or recordings by garage bands with the theme. One 45 took me fifteen years to get.

Q: So then you chase after the more original items?

MD: Yes, I love the one of kind stuff more, but I love it all. I'll take the manufactured piece or anything you may find in Grandma's attic.

Q: You also have four Woof Woof dolls?

MD: Yeah, a buddy of mine came into a grocery store where I worked and showed me the ad for them in a collector's magazine. I knew I had to have one and I saved up for it and sacrificed for it. Eventually I ended up getting four over the years. They were well worth it.

Q: What's your prized possession?

MD: The Herman paint by numbers set and the personalized stuff that was made for me or given to me by my friends.

Q: Okay Mark, we know you have an obsession with Lily. (Laugher) Why your obsession with Lily?

MD: I guess it starts back to when I was a kid. I always loved Lily and not Marilyn. When I became older I had his thing for goth girls and I guess I got it from Lily. I never met her but in the '90s I drove up to Boston to see her at a show, but she had to cancel out. I was disappointed but I did see the other cast. As far as Lily is concerned, I don't know...... there's just something about her.

Al Lewis as Grandpa Munster for a McDonald's campaign with other TV icons.

119

always loved the show, and going to the set and being tossed onto Fred's shoulders are wonderful memories. I have grown up with a fondness for monsters in general (although Frankenstein is the closest to my heart). Having Wolfman and Mummy heads around the house were not uncommon, nor was a green pointed ear on the coffee table. I am sure what would seem strange in most homes was very everyday normal in ours.

I must say we have a very interesting family tree, but being Butch's little sister was by far the most notable. It seems my name was actually "Eddie Munster's Sister" for years. I can't remember ever meeting anyone who has not seen the show and loved it. That's really the thing...Everyone always tells me how much they loved The Munsters, that it is a great childhood memory. There have been so many shows that have come and gone, shows that have been on television for decades but I believe few fans are as loyal as the Munster fans. Going with Butch to the many shows and conventions is always such a good time. I have met so many really wonderful people and none enjoy their fans more than my brother. I am always impressed with his genuine interest and appreciation of the people that come to see him. The recurring "where's Wolfie" question always brings a smile to our faces. I actually had him on my bed for years...not a teddy bear or a doll, I had Woof Woof in his faded green pajamas with the little bat logo on his chest...adorable.

I have three brothers and I am the only girl in the family, so I rather enjoyed the episode where Butch turned into Kimberly Beck. For some reason that one stands out, as do many others. I loved watching the one with our stepfather Kenny Hunt, when he played baseball (or tried to) with Herman. There really are so many, and I can't think of one I didn't like, but some just come to mind immediately...the episode where he ran away and wouldn't come down from the tree...the camping trip...Zombo...the Creature...all great.

We have had fun and made amazing memories to last a lifetime and I hope we keep making more of them for a long time to come.

- Michele, Butch's sister

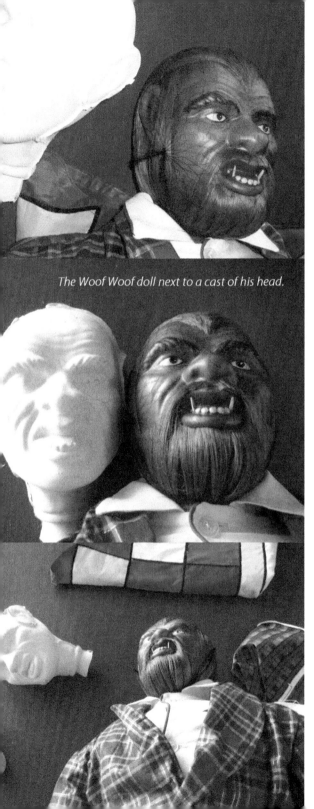

The Woof Woof doll next to a cast of his head.

OH WOOFY!
INTERVIEW WITH JIM MADDEN

Question: So Butch and yourself came up with the idea of creating a limited edition set of the Woof Woof dolls?

JIM MADDEN: Right.

Q: Can you talk about how you came up with that idea, and maybe a little about yourself?

JM: I went to California, to the Movieworld museum in Buena Park, the Cars of the Stars museum, and they closed the place down and had an auction at the Ambassador Hotel. They had a lot of movie memorabilia, and in the auction was Eddie Munster's chain bicycle, so I went there with a buddy and I ended up buying it. I wanted more information on the bicycle, so I tracked down Butch.

Q: So are you talking about the original bicycle from the series?

JM: That is a myth. The bicycle was given to Butch by Universal Studios, but was never shown on any episodes.

Q: But they did do publicity shots with it?

JM: Yes. When you look at the show, and keep looking for it, your mind goes nuts and you could swear you've seen it on the show. Anyway, after I bought the bike, I wanted some information on it, so I called Butch and we talked on the phone. He said he had relatives in the Phoenix area, and that he knew all about the bike. We arranged for him to come out and spend a day or so and tell me everything about it. He also mentioned that he had the Woof Woof doll, what was left of it anyway, since it was partially destroyed. When he came out, he brought the doll and I asked him if it would be for sale and he said he might consider selling it. So a couple days later, he called me and said he would sell it. I bought the

121

doll, but Butch wanted some kind of doll to replace it. We came up with an idea to restore that doll and make a limited edition version. We made a mold and casting, using the head from the original doll- the one and only from the show- and duplicated it. We then decided to sell the dolls.

Q: So you guys formed a partnership?

JM: The partnership with the doll was Butch and I. He would act as a salesperson. He would make sales calls and help me with whatever I needed. I want to say that Butch was extremely cooperative with me to the point where he would do anything he could to help. Whatever I asked him to do. To me, he was really goodhearted about the whole thing, and he really worked hard to promote the sales of the dolls whenever he could.
I came up with a few novel ways to sell the dolls. When Butch was being interviewed on TV, he'd take a doll with him and we'd occasionally get more money for the doll due to the fact that it was on national TV. Along with the doll, we would include several autographed photos and they could call me or write me. We would also have Butch call the customers and personally thank them on the phone. We included memorabilia photos with a biography of Butch, a list of the different articles about the dolls that were sold, and we would do the whole package and give them to the customers. The dolls were very, very costly because of the detail of each one.
One time we made arrangements for fans to have a personal audience with Butch - sort of a backstage type thing.

Q: What's your background? Had you had any previous experience with toy manufacturing or casting?

JM: No. Basically, I was born in Chicago and moved to Arizona when I was twenty-three or twenty-four. I worked in construction, some contracting and things like that. I got involved in a little bit of this and that, mainly go-carts. We moved to Hawaii and opened a go-cart racetrack and we were there for quite a while. Then, five years later, I came back from Hawaii and bought another track, seven or eight total in my career.

Q: Where did the original doll come from?

JM: I understand that the original doll was bought at a toy store. They used a JoJo the Monkey Doll. It had little bananas in one hand. This was the only one they used for the show. They took the original head off of the doll that they bought, and they made the new latex face that they used on the show. I know exactly what it looked like because I own an original doll. The only thing we changed was JoJo. He had these latex shoes that were sewn into the legs [that] were popular with dolls in the sixties. Like little molded tennis shoes. We couldn't replicate those, so we

cast little feet and hair. We bought little kid shoes or baby shoes to put on top of those feet. On those feet we painted the toenails black. Most of the customers were so sassy, they'd take the shoes off to see the little black toenails *(laughter)*. When some people saw our doll they were occasionally confused, because they assumed the original doll was brown, when it was actually green. Everybody except Marilyn was one shade of green or another on the show, including Woof Woof. People thought because the show was in black and white that the doll was brown. It was a misunderstanding, but I got a sixteen-millimeter print copy of the movie Munster, Go Home!, and the customers all got copies of two scenes in the movie so they could see where the doll was clearly green in color.

Q: Is the same doll for the series, or do you think they might have just made it for the movie?

JM: It's the same doll. They only made one doll.

Q: Did Butch have the doll all those years?

JM: The story of how Butch acquired that doll is this. Years later, he was at Universal and a makeup man said, "I've got something for you," and he went down to this file and in the bottom drawer was Woof Woof, and he gave it to Butch. Basically, the only part of the doll left was the head. The original doll had two little plastic nubs because in one episode it cried and they pushed water out of the eyes.

Q: How did your dolls originally come?

JM: Each doll was a limited edition. Each one was hand made, and along with the doll came a set of proper clothes.

Q: So how did you go about making the doll? There are usually challenges to this kind of project, as well as setbacks…

JM: The original doll was a miniature version of Lon Chaney, Jr. from Universal's The Wolf Man movie. We commissioned a lady who won many contests here and in Europe to create a firm body that was exactly like the body of the original doll. We made each part of the dolls from one master piece. We had to build settings and it would come out of the mold and we stitched it down like a professional doll. We also made the plaid pajamas and we also made a tweed suit with a shirt like the original doll, and I was almost fanatical in trying to reproduce it exactly. To this day, it is so obvious that people made attempts to reproduce this doll, but our doll is the authentic Woof Woof doll. My biggest disappointment was the hair. The original doll was built at Universal Studios. It was a latex head, and all sorts of hair was implanted into the scalp. In fact, it was glued on at the forehead line and you could see where the glue kept the hair in place. We couldn't get that exact. We used a rubber compound that was in a powder form that was put into the casting. That compound and the paint that we used for some reason didn't like each other, 'chemically speaking'. They would cause little cracks in the paint, so that would cause a problem on the head with the texture. The reason we did that was because that's the way the original doll was.

Q: I've actually seen the ones Mark (Marky Munster) Doyle has.

JM: Mark Doyle, he's one of my biggest customers (laughter)! He owns four. I think it was three from me and I think he bought one from some other person. So it was a long, long experience selling those dolls over a long period of time. The last dolls we sold towards the end must have cost us $1,395.00 apiece to produce. We had one doll that was sold in Florida that Disney had in their Epcot store for $5,000.00 resale. We had several sell for

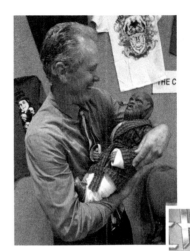

Ron Chaney, Nancy Allen and Dee Snider with Woof Woof.

$3,000.00 apiece. We have dolls in Germany, Japan and Austria.

Q: Any celebrity owners?

JM: A few celebrities. We can't prove it, because it was bought through someone else for Michael Jackson, but he got a doll. Bob Hoskins, who just recently passed away, got a doll. Several New York DJs, they got dolls. There's a big company called Billiken Toys in Japan that makes Godzilla merchandise. The United States representative reserved a doll, so he has one. There's a music group called Matchbox 20. They bought one. The dolls took on a life of their own and it became a popular item all by itself. They have been turned around and sold on the internet and they've all brought in more money then their original price. And people who have them, they just adore them.

Fred Gwynne pretends to give the original
Woof Woof a haircut.

125

My memories of The Munsters! Listing to Herman
do his jokes and hanging out with Grandpa in the lab.
-*Linda Kingston (Lancaster, California)*
    The dungeon was the best set in the house. Thanks!

The episode where Eddie wrote the report in blood!
That was pure metal!!!!
-*Arnold H.*
    Funny how certain things still stand up.

I believe Herman and Lily were the first to shack up
in a bed on TV!!
-*Barbara R*
    I think so!

Spot always eating the neighborhood cars!!
I always wanted Spot as a pet.
-*Mark D.*
    *Especially liked your car. Spot was great comedy
fodder for scripts.*

Eddie, stop biting your nails!!!
-*Gordon K.*
    *Funny one-those scenes were part of the success
many times over.*

Eddie's nickname was brilliant!! Loved the beard!!
-*Hayden C.*
    *Yeah, Paule Lynde made the show, plus my opening
rant which Herman ignores. Itchy beard.*

Zombo!
-Lizzy S.

> *Best episode ever! At least one the top five.*
> *Louie Nye was just hilarious.*

My entire life, I've been told I look like Eddie Munster. It's a handle I earned as a result of having a widow's peak, thick black eyebrows and hair, the fact that my name is "Ed," etc. I finally had a chance to meet Butch this weekend at Amazicon in Essington, PA and it was a dream come true. Such a nice guy and absolutely hilarious! All the best, Butch!
-Ed Danielov

> *Ed's your name and the hairline? OMG! Poor guy.*

I remember watching The Munsters in reruns in the '70s. It was a thrill to watch. When I got to meet Al Lewis at a convention in NYC, it was an even bigger thrill. I didn't think he would sign an autograph,so I purchased a pre-signed photo. Then when I found out he was signing, I stood in the long line. When Al looked at my photo and saw that it was already signed, I said, "Just write my name on it," and he did! Then, many years later, at the 2012 Monkees convention, I met Butch Patrick, who I so much wanted to meet! I still watch and enjoy The Munsters on DVD, and still laugh at the same jokes and antics. Long live the Munsters!
-Darrin Daniels (Pennsauken, New Jersey)

> *Glad we met...Thank you for being a Monkees*
> *and Munsters fan.*

Back in New York City in the 1950s, my uncle Jerry LaRocco, along with Al Lewis and Sidney Poitier, went to the Paul Mann Actor's Workshop, which was founded in 1953. Al and my uncle Jerry became good friends. Years later, my uncle had moved out to Los Angeles to pursue acting. Around 1961 or so, Al was called to do a pilot for a strange new show called The Munsters. Prior to going out to L.A. for the pilot, Al needed a place to stay while out there. So not really knowing anyone (else), he called my uncle and asked if he could stay at his place while filming the pilot. "Of course" was the answer, so Al flew out to the West Coast. Upon arriving at Jerry's apartment, Jerry said, "As a matter of fact, here's the key to the place. I'll be staying at my girlfriend's apartment. Use the place as long as you need it." So Al Lewis stayed there while filming the pilot for the Munsters. Fast forward to 1968. I was 10 years old. I wanted to visit my uncle. Actually, I had two uncles there. Jerry is my Father's brother. And Teddy was my Mother's brother. Both were actors in Hollywood, and good friends. So, at 10 years old my father put me on my first plane ride alone from NY to LA. He knew a stewardess who would look after me on the plane, and my uncles met me at the airport. Since I loved The Munsters so much, and I knew Al and Jerry were friends, naturally I wanted to meet "Grandpa". I hounded my uncle to meet him. Jerry Called Al, and arranged for us to go spend an afternoon at his home. We arrived there in the afternoon, and I met his wife Marge and his 3 sons, Ted, Dave, and Paul. We had lunch there and I played football on the front lawn. I can remember Al sitting in a big chair in his living room, with a big cigar, watching sports on television. Jerry chatted with Marge in the kitchen, while the kids played outside. We ended our visit with a picture of Al and me on his front stoop. A memory that will last forever. In 2010, I contacted Butch Patrick online. I told him about my "Grandpa Al" story, and we became friends too. Although we haven't met yet, we speak on the phone occasionally and keep in touch through facebook. Butch sent me an autographed picture, which I proudly display in my living room. I love the Munsters, and as an interior designer I've incorporated a Munster theme with their family pictures around my home. I feel this continues and completes a circle of Munsters in my life. My Uncle, Al Lewis, Butch, and me!

-Jay Lawrence

Thank you Jay. Good Stuff!
You're a great fan.

MY FONDEST MEMORIES WITH BUTCH PATRICK
BY CINDY LEGGETT

Michael Westmore and Butch.

My fondest memories started when first meeting Butch. I decided to attend a party in Austin that two friends of mine were hosting who were kings of the local cable world. They had a show called "Gesundheit" (1987) featuring all of the latest MTV Headbangers Ball videos and had great plans to expand. Their show was oddly familiar to the Saturday Night Live skit "Wayne's World", and to this day I believe that SNL actually acquired a lot of material and ideas from my two friends Clint and John. But, maybe for the time that was the norm and every young man's dream was to have a successful television and music cable program.

So there I was, knocking on Clint and John's door, ready to join the party. Butch opened the door and welcomed me inside and, honestly, I had no idea who he was. I was born and raised as an Air Force brat in Germany and the AFN TV Network never purchased any shows that he appeared in, including The Munsters. I had no clue. After a crazy night and much socializing, Butch decided to show me his motorcycle. At the time, he was commuting around Austin on a Kawasaki 550 and he thought it was cool that a chick had riding experience. I happened to be in one of those moods where I decided to take his keys from him,

jumped on his bike, and just drove off. Don't know what I was thinking or how he felt about it since only meeting me a few hours before, but I took a cruise and was gone for quite some time, before returning his bike and going back to the party. I had to laugh. No dings, no scratches, everything was fine. Butch couldn't believe it either. That was the start of a very special and long friendship that has lasted over 25 years.

Fast forward to a couple years later. There I was, living in Los Angeles, CA! I decided to make that big move to pursue a career in music management. I already had over 5 years experience in radio broadcasting having worked at 3 great FM Stations in Austin, plus band management skills, and wanted to make that "California dream" come true. I was given an open invite from Warner Bros. Records to pursue a career with their artist relations, marketing, and promotions teams in Burbank, CA. And oh, what a fun gig! Mo Ostin was at the helm of the organization and life was good. It felt great, and the record industry was still in its heyday. Butch was also becoming a very dear friend and his family had positively

Cindy with crew members of the Enterprise.

embraced me, and it was wonderful to know someone in LA who had lived in the area for their entire life.

One day I was processing promotional material for Cheap Trick's new upcoming tour and new album "Woke Up With A Monster," when Robin Zander, Tom Petersson, Rick Nielsen and Bun E. Carlos all walked past my desk. They stopped in midstride and turned around to look at Butch's picture on my desk. It was the greatest moment in my life. Tom blurted out, "Hey! He's my Astral Twin!" We laughed and then started chatting up a storm. They asked when I was going to see Butch next because they wanted to invite him to their show in San Diego the following week. I said he would definitely be there! The band then signed a band promo picture for me to give to Butch, and Tom signed it "To My Astral Twin. " It truly doesn't get any better than that. I love those guys! Rock n' roll forever.

Cable radio in Los Angeles used to be a really big deal before SIRIUS and XM Satellite Radio sliced into that market. FM Radio stations in general had been hit with a maelstrom of changes in the '90s, but Butch and I decided to do a show anyway since we loved the medium so much. Butch has always been a great announcer. His voice is perfect for radio, and I had 5 years experience in a studio production and running a board, so we made a great team and developed an hour-long heavy metal show that was incredibly fun. My fondest memory of the 2 years we were on the air at 99 Rock KCLA FM was in 1993. We were rocking the airwaves at a studio on Sunset Blvd. Bands were in and out as our live guests and the craziness never stopped.

In 1993, Butch decided I needed a tour of the Paramount Studios. He wanted to go visit his old friend and makeup artist Michael Westmore, who did his makeup on The Munsters at Universal Studios. Michael, being such a brilliant makeup artist, was hired by Paramount to do all of the makeup for various Star Trek productions, winning numerous Emmy Awards. Butch knew that I was a huge Star Trek and Star Trek Next Generation fan, and the invitation was an incredible treat, so I decided to ditch work and accompany Butch on this wonderful little adventure. When we got to the studio, Michael greeted us with a fabulous smile and asked if we wanted a tour of the U.S.S. Enterprise. OF COURSE we did!!! Who wouldn't want a tour of the famous starship. This was something I really wasn't expecting. I was on cloud nine

and couldn't stand the excitement. We left the makeup trailer to walk into the main film studio and the feeling was unbelievable. Here I was, a little ol' gal from Austin getting ready to have my picture taken in Capt. Picard's chair on the Bridge. OMG!! Does it get any better than that??!!

When we got back to the makeup trailer, Michael had to get one of the Ferengi ready for the next taping. I was completely enthralled with the process. The Ferengi and Borg designs were both developed by Michael and it was such an honor to have been there to

Cindy at a certain Captain's trailer.

witness the time and patience it took for an actor to sit there and be transformed into a legendary character. Michael pointed out the mask on the shelf above him that he had sculpted and created for Mick Fleetwood, of '70s rock band Fleetwood Mac fame, when the musician wanted to come to the show and be an alien in an episode on the second season. He was cast as an Antedean dignitary that was a fish-headed alien. Truly a masterpiece, amazing work! With Butch playing catch-up with Michael since they hadn't seen each other in several years, I was busy sparring with the Ferengi, who kept asking me if I had any money as he was keeping in character. I decided to step outside for a moment and take a peek to see if anyone else was coming to the trailer to have their face immortalized, when I bumped into a certain starship Captain. There was the Captain of the Enterprise just staring at me. I happened to have my camera in hand and politely asked him if I could take his picture. He blurted out in his classic British accent, "You most CERTAINLY may NOT!! Young lady, what are you doing with this camera on the studio lot???!!!!!!!!!" I started apologizing profusely and scuttled back into the makeup trailer. At that point Butch and I busted into pieces. The laughing didn't stop. That was truly a classic moment! Who better than the Captain of the U.S.S. Enterprise to scold me and become upset with me? I was in heaven. A day I will never forget.

In 1994, I decided I was going to marry my long-time boyfriend who I had met in Austin many years before. One of my fondest memories was when I decided to plan the wedding in Texas and I asked Butch if he would fly in to be a witness to a beautiful outdoor wedding ceremony at Zilker Park. He said "yes" and it was a very special and fantastic day for everyone. We decided to forego the traditional best man and maid of honor line up. It was a simple, elegant and fun wedding in the Asian gardens, and when the reverend asked who was going to witness this unity, Butch stepped up and said he was our witness and signed our marriage certificate! Now that's an autograph - Eddie Munster signing your marriage certificate. It doesn't get any better than that. He's an amazing person and a wonderful friend.

In 2001, I had already moved on from music and had been working at the Walt Disney Company for 2 1/2 years, employed at Disney Feature Animation in production. I became close friends with several of the artists that I oversaw, and they were very interested in my longstanding friendship with Butch. He was a "Munster" after all. The artists were always watching old TV shows, sketching crazy new concepts and dashing off to COMIC-CON every year. One day Butch called me and said he had purchased a new vehicle that I needed to see. I went to his house and, lo and behold, there was the original Grateful Dead tour bus sitting in his driveway. My reaction was, "So, when are we going for a ride?" I couldn't wait. Butch needed to do some minor repairs first and wanted to do a promotional event driving the bus through Los Angeles, sort of a party on wheels. I suggested that he invite a bunch of animators and rollout the promotion that way, since he had a built-in fan base where I worked.

It couldn't have been a more memorable day. Butch hired his neighbor to drive the bus and then drove into Burbank to pick up 10 animators for this experimental road trip. I don't think anyone knew what to expect, but just being inside this amazing mural painted bus with '60s and '70s posters of performances at Woodstock, Altamont, Monterey Pop Festival, The Avalon and The Fillmore glued to the inside roof was just utterly mind blowing. The artwork was inspiring and the animators loved it! We had no pre-set destination in mind, and it was better that way, so we decided to head into the Valley and then jump over the mountains from the 101 into Malibu. The jokes were flying and the cameras were filming and the weather had finally cooled down. When we got to the ocean, we needed to take a quick break while on the PCH to take in some cool ocean breeze and get out to stretch before moving on.

Butch in the makeup room while a Ferengi gets made up.

Bleary-eyed, we pulled over to a gas station in Malibu to use the restroom and fill up. The bus was so incredibly unusual looking on the outside, and we attracted quite an audience of partying residents that lived in the area. As we were loading up with snacks, 3 curious youngsters decided to board the bus with us to get a closer look. The reaction was priceless.

Our next stop was Hollywood and the Sunset Strip. By the time we got there, the traffic was already gridlocked. That didn't stop us, though. What a great night to be attracting attention with the Grateful Dead tour bus! I felt like I was in a remake of Cheech and Chong. If anything, the curbside audience and people in their vehicles were really digging it and the party vibe was everywhere. The Whisky, The Viper Room, The Roxy and The Key Club- all attention left the venues to follow the bus on the strip, and the party just kept rolling. My belly hurt from laughing so hard. I couldn't have asked for better company that night with Butch's introduction to some of the most creative people in LA. We all made it home safely and it was a night the animators will always remember. They were happy to have been a part in celebrating and exposing a piece of rock n' roll history. They were very gracious and thankful to Butch for such a great life's experience, and so was I.

Butch and Cindy on the bridge of the Enterprise.

I was born in 1961. During my elementary school days, I would run home from school to watch my favorite shows; Bewitched, I Love Lucy, I Dream of Jeannie, Hazel, Addams Family, Family Affair, and of course MY FAVORITE - The Munsters! I adored Herman, thought Marilyn was so pretty, was afraid of the pet dragon, and could especially relate to you (Eddie) because of your hairline. Being blessed with a widow's peak, there were many comments made about my hair by family, friends, and strangers alike. I was not able to have bangs (they would poof up & out). Well, for some reason, due to this, I could relate to Eddie - same forehead, kind of! Kids identify with certain things. They're silly and unpredictable (at least I was, and still am). Anyway, how in the world could I imagine how your character felt, being a girl growing up in a middle-class suburb of Chicago? One will never know, but I still get warm fuzzy feelings recalling all of the crazy antics during the episodes of your show. Your television family was, and remains, a part of my imaginary family, fostering fond childhood memories! Thank you Butch Patrick...

-Deb Carpenter Grant *(Troy, Ohio – formerly from Arlington Heights, Illinois)*

WOW! PB & J and Ovaltine..My favorite too! Thanks so much for the memory.

I had always known The Munsters growing up. I'd watch it after The Monkees were on in the afternoon on a channel that showed older TV shows. Slowly, they stopped showing it and I grew older. When I was 19, getting ready to have my son, my brother Dusty played 'Munster, Go Home!' for everyone on the DVD player. I'm not sure why, but it made me hysterical to the point where I started having Braxton Hicks (contractions) and was rushed to the hospital. The next day my son Poncho was born. I always thought that was the only Munsters "experience" we'd have. Flash Forward 6 years to early one day in early September, 2011. I'm sitting in my mom's (who was a professor) office and she runs through the door and announces "EDDIE MUNSTER IS ON HIS WAAAAY!!" I said, "That's nice" and went back to typing my papers, thinking a long haired Rob Zombie-type would waltz through her door and blow us all off and act like he was performing some sort of blessing by being there. But instead, this guy who's clean, wearing a Munsters t-shirt and jeans, walked in and introduced himself, smiling at everyone. After getting to know Butch better, we struck up a friendship and he began taking me to his conventions. Just getting to see how many people smile and want to hug him and thank him for his show is instantly contagious, and I find myself smiling just as big as the fans as they share their stories about the Munsters. I am blessed to have someone who is my best friend. He brings so much happiness and compassion to his fans that it is almost unbelievable.

-Manda Murphy

My favorite memory of that wonderful show was that being the youngest of three, my older brother would pick on me consistently. But I would get my revenge! As soon as the program came on, I would hum the theme over and over and that would drive him crazy! It was one of the few times I would get into his craw.

-Larry Kaiser (Lincolnwood, Illinois)

As far back as I can remember, the Munsters have been a part of my life. I was born in August 1964, just in time to watch them, and they have been a big influence on me and have cheered me up many times. Now that I'm 49 years old, I realize its okay to be different. I play guitar and sing in a band and have overcome the shyness I had as a kid thanks to The Munsters. I also play a zombie at the local haunted house every October. I have a 1932 Ford coupe rat rod and am into hot rodding and pinstriping, all because of my days as a kid watching the Munsters Koach and Dragula. I will always love The Munsters-until I'm 150 and forever!
-Ritchie Sabin (Elmira, New York)

Glad we could be there for you.

My favorite memory was the cars.
God love the cars,
and the go cart too!
-Thomas L.
*Favorite scenes are always
with the Koach!*

A publicity photo for "The Munster" Car Coat (1965).

"Herman's Plaster Head"

My memory of the Munsters began nearly 36 years ago and was career altering. It was August 1977 and my 13th birthday had just passed. Armed with a pocket full of cash, I rode my bike up to the main road of our subdivision. On the corner was a plaster craft store called Art Accent. Already loving Halloween, and with the haunting season just around the corner, I went in looking for anything creepy to scare the trick or treaters that would visit our house that Fall. In the Holiday section, to my shock, was the most wonderful thing my eyes could handle. A white plaster head of Herman Munster! I grabbed it like I'd just found a gold nugget. Paid for the Herman head along with 2 shades of green, black, and red paint. I rode home and immediately began my artistic work! No doubt some art center would want this head to display and no doubt nobody had ever chosen the hideous green that I had selected. It was a masterpiece! I could not wait to show it off that Halloween.

Later that year I would acquire a big black buzzard from an abandoned carnival ride. His head turned back and forth on an electric motor. At the same time, my school was clearing out their seasonal decoration room and gave me a broken Victorian girl. The Victorian girl was supposed to be decorating a Christmas tree, she had a motorized head too. I removed the head and made the perfect grave prop. With all this I began early the morning of October 31st, 1977 decorating my front yard. The Herman head was placed in the big front window of our house for all to see! It was much too valuable to be placed outside. That past Christmas the neighborhood thugs had stolen every Christmas light bulb, within reach, from my holiday lights display and smashed them in the street. The thought of them doing the same to my Herman Munster head was unthinkable. I could not allow that pack of wolves the pleasure of smashing this plaster work of art on the streets of our neighborhood. I built a path using old fencing and leaves that forced the kiddies to walk right past the Herman Munster head safely displayed in our front window. And they loved it!

My yard was such a hit that year that I decided to build a haunted house in our garage the following year.

When Halloween 1978 arrived, I began filling my haunt with the best of the best. This included my precious Herman head. It was time for him to go on display in a more personal surrounding. For admission I was charging 25 cents per person so I had to give the best show possible. In the last room, right before they would exit, I placed the Herman head on a shelf with a green blinking light to enhance his green face. My Haunted House was a big success. It set the course for many, many years to come.

37 years later with 14 haunted houses under my belt, I now realize it all began with the painted Herman Munster head from the plaster store purchased with birthday money. I now run the Baxter Avenue Morgue in downtown Louisville, my largest haunt yet. I no longer use the Herman head in my commercial displays but you will find him in our living room at home, in our best china cabinet, placed proudly right next to my wife's fine china and glassware. By the way, my wife is not as pleased as I am with my green hand-painted plaster Herman Munster head.

-Jamie Stephenson
(Louisville, Kentucky)

True one, there's always a solution. Good memories, my friend!

I didn't get THE MUNSTERS until I left home for college. Both literally and figuratively, I didn't get them. When I was a kid growing up none of the TV stations in my hometown's viewing area had the Universal/MCA syndication package, so we never saw LEAVE IT TO BEAVER, THE MUNSTERS, THE DONNA REED SHOW, or FATHER KNOWS BEST. I never got to be immersed in THE MUNSTERS in the same way a lot of the people I know now as an adult did. I saw Butch Patrick in the network kids shows he did in the 70s (and I was a huge fan) and I knew Fred Gwynne from his kids' books (loved THE KING WHO REIGNED) and Al Lewis from old movies he'd been in. On those rare occasions that we were traveling and THE MUNSTERS was on TV, I understood the concept but didn't understand what it was really making fun of, although I remember knowing the show was funny nevertheless. If you haven't seen traditional family sitcoms like DONNA REED or BEAVER, one can't even see how MUNSTERS is poking fun at them from the opening credits. It was when I got to university and had a full immersion in that stuff, **then** MUNSTERS really takes off and is incredible. You have the amazing chemistry between Lewis and Gwynne and the impeccable straight-man timing of Yvonne DeCarlo, so the jokes work, but you have no idea exactly how subversive that family is (maybe even more so than THE ADDAMS FAMILY who never even so much as tried to fit in). The sweetness and positivity that Butch and Pat bring to the package just make it all so much better. This gets nuttier when the series goes on to its second season and even starts to make fun of itself. I also loved the clearing house of great guest appearances the show seemed to have in people like Jesse White, Bonnie Franklin, Zalman King, Frank Gorshin or John Carradine. Favorite moments include Lily smuggling Grandpa out of the dormitory as her wolf stole, any scene with Al Lewis in the drag-strip episode, the moment when Herman realizes that Lily isn't attracted to him anymore when he looks human, and Lily getting down with a folk-song to a crowd of beatnik Standells fans after Herman has blown their minds with an impromptu free form slam poetry recitation. "Scooba-Doo and Scooba-Die – That chicken ain't too young to fry" is still one of the funniest things I've ever seen in my life.

Joe Kilmartin is a Toronto Canada area actor and writer who has a love for monsters and popular culture. You can read his reviews at http://we-love-monsters.com or in the magazine of that name. He is usually found jabbering like a pundit or speaking about himself in the third person. Photos by Krissy Myers.

The Munsters are referenced every time I get my haircut. I have a widow's peak, and if my hair is cut too short it really stands out. I say "Don't cut it too short in the front. If you cut it too short, I end up looking like Eddie Munster."
-Michael Marquis (Indianapolis, Indiana)

What's wrong with that?

I did get to speak to Mr. Patrick when he visited radio station WZZO in Allentown, Pa. The story I have involves "Eddie's" hair, specifically the front point. My son at an early age had somewhat of a point also. His mother did not want her son to look like Eddie, so she trimmed and shaved that spot until it was less obvious. She did this for quite some time. Both the point and, sadly, Eddie went away. I don't believe my son knew why this happened at the time. Thanks for the laughs.
-James McCaughin (Center Valley, Pennsylvania)

Always the hairline. Love the car too.

I have a lot of great memories of the Munsters. I don't know if I can pick out one favorite. I really liked when Herman was a rock star, when he was on the Russian sub, and the episode with Zombo. Any episode with Jessie White as a guest star was good.
-John Snyder (Germantown, Ohio)
Good Choices All...Lots of timeless comedy episodes.

Best episode is "A House Divided"!!
-Derry R.

Funny doesn't describe the antics of that episode.

Bill and I do a theme every Halloween, and one year it was The Munsters. Bill as Herman, me as Lily, and even our dog Shayna was Spot. We have a 1928 Model A Ford, currently being rebuilt into a RatRod. We dragged it out to the front, decked it out in cobwebs, and made our own Munster Koach! The house was spooky in all it's Munster decorations, right down to 1313 Mockingbird Lane (even had the clock) and Herman's lunchbox! Needless to say, we were the stars of the block once again.
-Karen Stretch (Niagara Falls, New York)

Excellent!

I remember being little and watching Munsters reruns on TV, and I always thought they were so much fun and so cool. They always stuck with me and turned me into a huge fan years later. I was an eccentric kid who always liked things a bit off the beaten path -not to say The Munsters were on that path exactly, because they are a huge part of Pop Culture then, now and forever- but let's just say not too many kids my age sat around watching reruns of an old black and white TV show. Anyway, a Munster Memory that I truly hold dear to my heart was having dinner with my mother years later and watching those reruns all over again with her. I didn't realize how much of a fan of the show she had always been too. It was just another cool thing for us to share. I'd give anything to watch Herman and Lily with their crazy family alongside my mother again over dinner... Thanks for always keeping an open mind when it came to me, Ma. I know it was tough sometimes.
-Soda (New York, New York)

A very thoughtful memory. Thank you so much and thank Ma too.

I love Lily's hair. Having a background in hair and makeup, I can only imagine how much the wig weighed and how much work it took.
-Christy G.
It was very heavy. She had five people in her makeup and wardrobe department.

I love how they had black nail polish before it really was an "in thing".
Yep! Lily was the original "Goth" Mom!

My Favorite episodes were when Herman played sports, the Leo Dorosher episode where Herman wrecks the park. When he destroyed the golf course and buried Eddie up to his neck trying to get out of the sand trap. Fast motion was priceless. Herman and the spaceman on the walkie-talkie. Too many to name... Still laugh hard! That's how you can tell a classic.
-Scott Hurley

I agree, too many to name. At least 20 superb classics.

I think anyone that didn't love The Munsters was/is crazy. I love it because it was different. Totally outside the box for its time, yet it was perfectly executed, no crudeness and not offensive. Growing up, I never really fit in. We didn't have much money and I never really did what "everyone else" was doing. I was usually the weird one (before it was cool to be weird). =) The Munsters taught me that it was ok to be different. Eddie, Herman, Lily, Grandpa & Marilyn let me know that it was ok to be me. I may have been a quieter version back then, but I have always been me. And let's not forget to mention Spot, Woof Woof, the house, the car, Lily's clothes, Grandpa's lab, Herman's laugh..... PERFECTION! Thank you for all the wonderful childhood memories! =)
-Angie West (Cincinnati, Ohio)

Perfect memory Angie. Glad you watched us and loved the comparisons.

138

When Grandpa turned himself into a bat and Eddie traded him, I couldn't control my laughter!!!
-Timothy L.

My favorite line was " I swear the bat just fainted."

Loved the makeup!
-Adam W.
The BEST!

The Munsters was my favorite show when I was a kid and, thanks to Netflix, I still watch it every night before I go to bed! As a kid growing up in Wilmington, VT, I was a latch-key kid. I was left home after school, by myself, at a young age. Not un-common in the 60s! The Munsters was a great babysitter, and soothing for some reason, and I never felt alone. I also had Butch Patrick's photos on my wall, and over my bed, I had a giant door-size photo of Herman. It was plastic, with stick-on glow-in-the-dark eyes. I remember ordering it out of a comic book, and my friend and I wondering how big it would be! Of course, the comic book advertised it like it was a lot bigger, not the thin plastic poster that came, but it was life size, however, and looked great over my bed! I had a Munsters lunchbox as a kid, and I think it was my all-time favorite item I owned as a kid. Wish I had it now...not for the value, but for the childhood memories. As an adult, I still find The Munsters a soothing show to turn on at bed time. It reminds (me) of my childhood. Even though I spent a lot of time home alone, I was never really alone. I had Lily, Herman, Grandpa, Marilyn, and Eddie to keep me company!!!
-Brenda Shepard (Brattleboro, Vermont)

Wow you said it all. Thank you so much for a wonderful memory.

Eddie always climbing in and out of the chimney and cabinets. How did he do that?
-Misty R.

I was so small they wrote it in.

I raced home every day and to watch The Munsters! My family wasn't great, but the Munsters family was perfect in my eyes!
-Andy K.

Glad we were there for you.

Met Butch Patrick at The Monkees Convention. Awesome, down to earth guy. Had a great time chatting with him.
-Scott Murray (Turnersville, New Jersey)

Thanks Scott...Loved doing The Monkees Christmas Show.

I met Butch Patrick in August, 2013, at the 'Wheels of Time Street Rod Show' in Macungie, PA. I grew up watching The Munsters and was excited when I heard Butch was going to be at the car show. I've always been told that my 1927 Ford T-bucket looks like the Munsters' car. I've been in three Halloween parades as "The Munsters". At the first parade in 2006 (before car was painted black), we won "Best in Show" and a $100 prize. At the 2010 parade, we won a trophy for "Most Original". Butch was very friendly, posed with me and my car, and even autographed the dashboard!
- Gary Detweiler

Thanks Gary. Had fun there. Nice meeting you!

My memory will always be Herman's reacting to Eddie's fit. "Oh darling, I think Eddie's home!" Just the way he reacted to the tantrums of Eddie was great!!!
-Kim L

HA HA HA YEAH! He kept his thoughts on his newspaper.

You have to have such a wonderful feeling as to bring joy to countless millions of people. I'm 68, born and bred (in) Brooklyn. A gunshot wound as a ghetto street cop with the NYCPD left me with permanent nerve damage post-operative, but life went on. You and the beautiful cast you worked with were such a great experience to behold!

-Ralph Grosso (Carversville, Pennsylvania)
Looks like we both survived the sixties. Stay Strong!!!

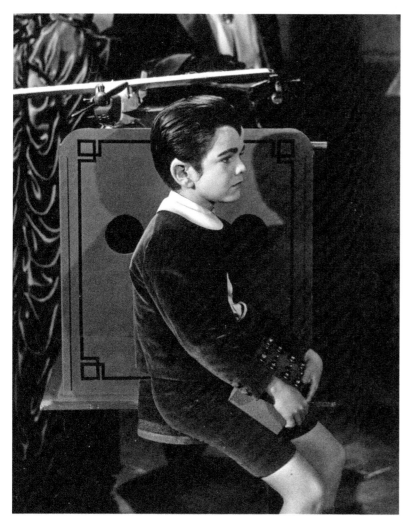

My friend Charline and a few of us would pretend we were characters from the show. We played in an old barn that was our "Munster House". I've met Butch at Charline's haunted garage. Cool guy!

-Bonnie McKnight (Ludlow Falls, Ohio)
I love her haunted garage!! Keith and Charlene are awesome!

141

I have been a lifelong fan of The Munsters. I've been collecting everything Munsters related that I can get my hands on for more than half my life...from toys, new and old, to tattoos that will last forever. So when my 4 year old daughter, Scarlett, picked up one of my Eddie Munster dolls with sincere excitement, getting ready to go meet Butch Patrick at Captain Chucks Comics in Baltimore, I was just so overwhelmed and proud. She's been raised on the Munsters, and even does the vintage jigsaw puzzles with me! She was so happy to meet him, I barely got a word in! But believe me, that was fine! She showed Butch the witch hat she insisted on wearing and the Eddie toy and babbled away. In fact, she was so excited we had to get back in line so she could also tell him "We watch the Munsters every day!" And that's no exaggeration! He was just such an absolute pleasure to meet! He even gave my mini Munster a free autographed picture. Meeting "Eddie Munster" was something so special that I got to share with my daughter, and an experience I will treasure forever.

-Kristina "Kreep" Pierce
(Silver Spring, Maryland)

Thank you for coming out. I had a blast and glad to have met you.

I completely relived my childhood when A & W brought the Munsters back for their Halloween advertising.
-Sean J.

Who better than us?

Lily was the most beautiful woman in the world!! Why people thought the blonde was the prettiest one, I'll never guess. Herman was a lucky man!!
-Martin T
Yes, Pop was very lucky.

My family played the game a lot.
-Susie C.
People still enjoy the memorbilia.

Carrying my lunchbox to school every day my third grade year.
-Kevin T.
Hope you still have it. Worth $$$$ with the thermos.

Uncle Gill was not only the creature from the black lagoon, but their uncle! That's awesome!
-Roger B.
All the Universal Monsters were awesome!

The outfits stuck out in the '60s, and the Munsters never cared!
-Adam E.
Trendsetting! We wore the same clothes except for Marilyn.

The cars made what I do today...Chop and redo cars!!!
-Danniel V.
Car shows are my favorite places to visit too.

Other than my favorite episode, "Hot Rod Herman", I have two stories. One, getting to stay home sick from school to watch The Munsters, and two, spending two days with Butch Patrick. He did his laundry at my house the day before an appearance at a friend's dealership with the replica Munster Coach and Dragula. We had dinner that night and then a radio appearance the next morning. Had a great time with a TV icon. Hope to do it again soon!!!!!
-Brian Rider (Bethlehem, Pennsylvania)

Hey Brian, thanks for the tell-all. I owe you one!

Eddie's baseball bat!!!
-Judy E.
The bat was heavy.

My favorite was Herman being kidnapped and being worshiped as the special one!
-Lena F.
The Russian fishing trawler.

Love the show! One of my faves is when Herman plays base-ball!
-Kathy Thacker (Amherst, Virginia)
Me too. My step dad actually played Pro Ball and was the catcher.

When I was 10 or so, I thought since my dad's name was Fred, he was related to all guys named Fred. And so I thought Fred Gwynne was my uncle. When I was 13, I met Butch at Robert E. Peary Junior High. By then I knew I wasn't related to "Herman", but I sure had a crush on "Eddie". Thanks for the memories, Butch.
-Freda Matkovitch (River Pines, California)

*Yup, coming back to Jr. High after the Munsters.
Good times for sure.*

144

Loved The Munsters series. Had the pleasure of meeting Grandpa (Mr. Lewis) when I was a kid. He used to sit in the area school playground (PS 84 NYC West 92 St.) on his time off from the series. Mr. Lewis would talk to all of us. He had a restaurant in the village, and when my niece met him (when she was 13 years old), he remembered my brother and I. "Oh, the twins from the school ground." He was very active in social causes in NYC. My husband and I were at a friend's apartment and Mr. Lewis was there. I approached him and he remembered me and talked to me for hours. He was a joy and I am so blessed I had the honor to have met him.

-Sandy Valles (New York, New York)
We were blessed to have him.

Keith and I were both fans of The Munsters, and since we were celebrating Lucky 13 in 2012 at The Haunted Garage (where all proceeds were given to fight Multiple Sclerosis), what better special guest victim than Butch Patrick! We contacted him, and Butch agreed to make the trip. He made a second visit in 2013, and we hope he makes it an annual visit. Great guy and fun to work with--THANKS from Haunted Garage and MS!!!

-Charline Werts and Keith Allen (Tipp City, Ohio)
Any time. Glad to help.

My favorite episode was when Herman needed a driver's license. He and Grandpa went to that little town called Groverville. The old man who was in charge of licenses was perfectly cast. Loved the eye exam. Old Man: "Can you see this chart?" Herman: "Yes." Old Man: "You passed."
-Andrew Hurwitz (Evanston, Illinois)
A great one.

Loved The Munsters! Watched it all the time. Cool to have a pet dragon under the stairs and a cool grandpa. Very entertaining show!

-Ray O. (Denver, Colorado)
Spot was cool and so was Grandpa.

145

To think a television program, that was made over the span of a mere two years, could have such a resounding impact on people's memories some fifty years later is an astounding thing. The Munsters are as alive and joyous as ever and have etched themselves into the collective conscious. Eddie has always been my favourite character, played with such tenderness by Butch Patrick. I first saw the Munsters in repeats on TV in Australia when I was around the same age as Eddie so felt an immediate affinity with him. As a visual artist I find myself continually drawn to things from my childhood for inspiration and the Munsters is one such treasured token.

Here is a drawing I made with ink and tea on paper in 2009 called 'Eddie Munster Vignette'.

Thank you for the pleasant screams!

-Paul Compton

Thanks, great art.

I first met Butch on the set of My Favorite Martian. I was his stunt double there for the first time. Throughout the years our paths crossed often. I was his double on The Munsters and worked with him again on Lidsville the summer of '71. He always was fun to be around and as he says to me often, "I've known Felix longer than anyone in Hollywood." Glad to call you a friend, Butch.

-Felix Silla

Thanks, my friend.

When I first came to this country. The first television show I watched was The Munsters. I found it most profound.

-Cary Elwes

Glad you did, Cary.

MY MUNSTER MEMORY

BY RICHARD MAURIZIO

When has The Munsters affected my life? When hasn't it? Like a lot of us, I grew up with the show and remember coming home from school and watching The Munsters in the afternoon. I loved the antics of Herman and Grandpa and the situations they would get into and how they got out of them. As a child, the one thing The Munsters taught me (and also coming from a big Italian family) was that family is the most important thing and you stick together no matter what.

My favorite character is Herman and I can relate to him on so many different levels with the way he always tried to do different things. Even though he could be a bit childish at times, he was always a good father, which is most important to me in my own life. The one big memory for me of the show was the episode when Herman was drawing a description of himself. I'd always wanted to be a cartoonist, and when I saw Herman draw that picture I was like, "WOW! That is so cool." At one point in my life I did become a cartoonist, and Herman helped inspire me to follow my dream.

Fast forward to 1992, I was working on a magazine called Collectible Toys and Values. The theme for one of the issues was monsters, so I told the editor I wanted to do an article on The Munsters. I contacted Al Lewis at his restaurant Grampa's and asked if I could do an interview with him. He replied, " Sure, come on down." I went there with my Dad. My late father Alex Maurizio was a professional photographer and took photos of Al Lewis during the interview. (The photos and the interview are also in this book.) So we arrived at Grampa's and standing there was Grandpa Munster in a Cowboy hat! Didn't he wear a tuxedo?

While we were doing the interview, I felt like that child again who watched the show after school, sitting with Grandpa himself and talking about The Munsters. After the interview, he gave us dinner and to this day that was the best veal parmesan I've ever had in my life (sorry, grandma).

I've always been involved in comic books and I had one company in the '80s called Spotlight Comics. The idea for Spotlight was to publish comics based on cartoons and TV shows. We published Mighty Mouse and Underdog, and another artist suggested The Munsters. (Why I didn't think of that I don't know). I called Universal and almost had it in my hands.

We weren't able to come to an agreement at that time, but I gave it a second attempt in 1998 with TV Comics (later to be called Airwave Comics). We published I Dream of Jeannie, VIP, Mister Magoo's Christmas Carol, and of course The Munsters. While publishing this book I made a lot of friends, whom I remain friends with to this day, and also became friends with Butch Patrick. We did a nationwide tour together with Butch and Pat Priest and published a special issue for 1998 San Diego Comic-Con. Along with the Comic-Con edition, the book ran four issues, one trade paperback, and so many variant covers you could wallpaper a small room.

After the book, I would run into Butch at shows and we would hang out sometimes or go to dinner. In the beginning of this year Butch called me and asked if I wanted to work with him on a Munster Memories book. I told him of course.

My newest Munster memory is…while working on this book I was viewing all the episodes, and my eight-year-old daughter came over and wanted to know what I was doing. I told her that I was watching The Munsters, and she snuggled up next to me and we watched them together. She laughed at Herman and Grandpa's antics and we laughed together. I felt like that little child again watching my favorite show in the afternoon except years later with the one thing in life I cherish the most.

Thanks, Herman and my dad for showing me how to be a father. You both have Ward Cleaver beat.

- Richard Maurizio

I love The Munsters. It is so funny that it cracks me up. I love all the episodes. I can't choose my favorite. My favorite characters are Lily and Herman. I Like Lily cause she's pretty and Herman because he's funny.

Anna Mia Maurizio

MY MUNSTER MEMORY

BY BUTCH PATRICK

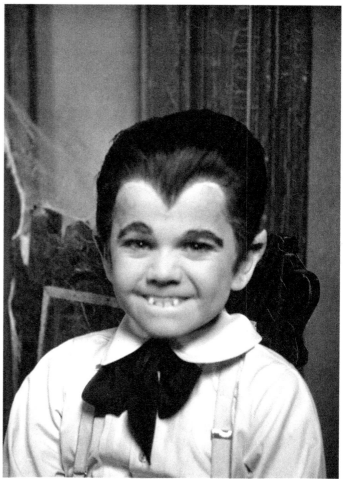

After reading and talking to thousands of people about THEIR Munster memories, it's kinda strange reflecting on the process myself. Without going into all the peripheral facts surrounding getting the part of Eddie, I'll just say briefly what one or two were the BEST memories. Actually, the job on the show wasn't the best memory at all. Good, you bet, but the truth is, being Eddie allowed me the freedom to experience the REAL treat!! Exploring the greatest backlot in Hollywood, or for that matter, the world. Over two years I got to know everyone and they let me be a boy, a boy who happened to be in green make-up, but a young kid who loved getting a firsthand look at the magic called movie making. Sure, on The Munsters we had great makeup, special effects, and plenty of stars as well, but with a dozen movies in production at any given time, I was allowed to poke around sets being built and broken down after the movies wrapped. My buddies were the behind the scenes artists and carpenters who make the awesome visuals we take for granted. Or the lighting techs who you'd never see because they were invisible high on the catwalks.

During lunch you'd see the likes of Charlton Heston, or Paul Newman and Lana Turner. It wasn't uncommon to see Bobby Darin dropping by to see his sweetheart Sandra Dee. Western stars like James Drury of the Virginian and Ward Bond, star of Wagon Train. Oscar winner Ernest Borgnine was one of my favorites out at the lagoon where McHale's Navy was stationed. Just google movies from 1964 to 1966 out of Universal Studios and you'll see the amazing list of stars I was able to see on a daily basis. But what no one will EVER know was how much fun was had by one Butch Patrick, and the memories of exploring Universal City Studios when he wasn't in school or on the set of his show called The Munsters!

Butch Patrick

Afterword

I'd like to express my sincere thanks to everyone who submitted their story. The memories they have shared with me were the basis for this book. The fans are the reason the shows are allowed to endure. I was lucky enough to fall into a dream job that allows me to have friends worldwide. The Munsters are a phenomenon. 50 years and going stronger than ever. New fans, old fans and in-between fans too! Researching and reconnecting with people responsible for the show and it's incredible longevity has been an honor. Many people are owed a special thanks. None more than my two best Munster buddies on the planet, Kevin Burns and Tony Greco. They generously shared not only their memories, but supplied me with never-before-seen pictures and info about their collections. Another thanks to Michael Westmore and George Barris and family. Without the makeup and the cars, we may have just been another "normal" average American family. Except for the great writing, music, guest stars, special effects, set design and a few other production departments, that is! They all worked together to bring the country The Munsters, a CBS Thursday night hit. It was a one of a kind show that today has stood the test of time. My favorite quote from a fan happens to be, "If I was stuck on a desert island with only one show to watch it would be The Munsters". Oh, by the way, I heard that when I was a guest on the Howard Stern show, by the host himself. In closing, my utmost thanks to Pat Priest for her participation, and finally to the writer, researcher, artist and my friend Rich Maurizio. He made sure this 18-month project was done in 6 months to coincide with the Sept 24 original air date. It actually WAS 50 years to the day when we finished this book. Here's to another 50 :-)

Thanks, **BP**

CPSIA information can be obtained
at www.ICGtesting.com
Printed in the USA
BVOW07s0630060716
454590BV00023B/219/P